I0531836

THE NEW FORGIVENESS

All rights reserved

Published by:
Global Vision Publishing
Fort Lauderdale, FL

Copyright © 2022 Caroline Pena

All rights reserved. No part of this book may be reproduced by any means, nor transmitted, nor stored in a retrieval system, nor translated into a machine language, in any form or by any means, electronic, mechanical, photocopying, recording, or otherwise, without the prior written permission of the author.

Caroline Pena • www.CarolinePena.com

Global Vision Publishing • www.GlobalVisionPublishing.com

Cover design: Tim Pedersen
Cover photo: Plumb Talk Productions
Editors: Tammy DiBacco and Carrie Lyons

Printed in the United States of America

ISBN-13: 979-8-9857948-7-8

My Dear Husband, Cesar,

I wrote this book in honor of the journey we have shared together. You have allowed me the time and space I needed to achieve one of the greatest gifts of all, forgiveness. Your patience, understanding and willingness to grow with me in our relationship has been an inspiration. You allow me to be myself, to achieve new heights and you catch me when I fall… every time.

When one says to a man that they are a great father, the energy of that is immense. I can never find the exact words to express the wonderment I have for you regarding the stellar father that you are, but I can say thank you beyond all measure, for my dear and beloved children, Maddox and Sarai. They are my precious and rare gems, and they love you as much as I do.

Your Affectionate Wife,
Caroline

Dear Reader,

It took me years to finally grasp the concept, idea, and knowledge that forgiveness is only for the person doing the forgiving. It took years of heartache and millions of tears to understand that forgiveness has nothing to do with the person or circumstance that hurt you so much. Forgiveness is a feeling, and it is a feeling that you get to have. It is a feeling inside of you, and when you achieve it, your entire body feels a freedom, a space that is now void of hatred and full of love. After an attack in my own home, I was left in a tangled web of resentment, fear and post-traumatic stress that shadowed every moment of my life for the years that followed. Over time I learned how to let go of my hatred and transform my experiences into the exact fuel I needed to achieve the joy, happiness, peace and success I so very much craved.

My mission is to open your mind and influence change, so you can use your thoughts and emotions to better serve you. I will explain what you have been told about your experiences and how they can affect your life in a much more meaningful way. My intention is to open your eyes and teach you how to use the power of the energy behind your emotions as the fuel and inspiration to transform any experience you've had in your lifetime, into something that serves you, and ultimately leads you to forgive. Imagine this: you know how to take the powerful emotion of hatred and transform that emotion from the energy it provides into the energy that is a driving force you can use to achieve anything, including forgiveness!

When you experience how this feels in your body, you will be forgiving faster, moving forward quicker, and experiencing simultaneous joy while doing it! Mastering this process is not easy, but with repetition and practice you absolutely can succeed. The better you get at it the happier your days will become. You will reclaim your personal power of joy and no one, and nothing, can take it away again.

You're in complete control of your happiness! This in no way means that sad, bad and horrible circumstances will not happen to you. On the contrary, these things will happen, without a doubt. I know life throws its curve balls, trust me, I do. You have heard that saying right? It is not what happens to you, it is how you overcome it, and how you choose to exist on the other side. Well, this book is here to teach you how to overcome it and how to transform energy into anything that will reestablish your inner peace and joy.

"*The New Forgiveness*" is an entirely new and revolutionary way to understand how experiences and the emotions they create are just energy. In fact, experiences are palpable, measurable energy. You will learn how to transform that energy into joy, by using it to instantly turn emotional pain into the fuel you need to heal your hurt and create a moment that propels you towards your dreams.

If you want to learn how to use that energy for yourself and the world around you in a positive and effective way then this book is for you. This book will teach you how to transform your hurt into forgiveness, and it will allow you to, in its utmost completion, reach and transcend your forgiveness journey.

Contents

"Happiness is letting go of believing you can have a better past."

-Caroline Pena

Serenity

Can you hear the sounds of life
Echoing in your dreams?
It's the light of knowledge
Which brings you here,
While you wonder if your path is near.

You've tainted hope but somehow found
A way to satisfy,
That saddened part of you
That so much wants to fly.

When in the morn, your eyes are thin
Just breathe throughout your day,
You'll not frown upon these challenges,
Just shine along the way.

The light you'll pass along
Will not come from you alone,
You'll have your joyful song
And your beauty will be shown.

"Caroline Pena"

The New Forgiveness

Foreward

The first time I sat down with Caroline Pena was at an oceanside restaurant in Lake Worth Beach, Florida. As she began to share her vision and stories for this book, I remember silently speaking to God, "Lord, I am humbled being in the presence of such a wondrous and magnificent soul, with a beautiful and powerful vision in her heart. This is going to be an adventure."

"Sometimes we think there's no way we can live with, or find peace with something that has happened, but we can. If you don't believe that, then the darker forces have you right where they want you. Forgiveness is possible." -Caroline Pena, The New Forgiveness.

I have literally sat with thousands of individuals and listened to their visions. But that precious afternoon I did something I had never done before. I reached into my briefcase and pulled out a notepad and sketched a drawing of Caroline. I'm not an artist of that kind, but I needed to draw what I was seeing in her face, body, and spirit as the sea breeze and waves moved behind her and through her. I knew it was a moment of destiny. Magnificent.

The New Forgiveness is a journey. Caroline Pena takes you on a journey of forgiveness, light, love, power, healing, miracles, freedom, and family. Her journey becomes your journey. Her forgiveness becomes your forgiveness. Her light becomes your light.

Her love becomes your love. Her power becomes your power. Her healing becomes your healing. Her miracles open space for your miracles. Her freedom becomes your freedom. And her family becomes your family too.

We are commanded in scripture to forgive our enemies and pray for those who persecute us. But how? The New Forgiveness gives us the pathway and actual proven tools to achieve this kind of true and lasting forgiveness.

Caroline's teaching and understanding of Energy: The Key to Unlocking Forgiveness, The Effect Emotions Have on Your Qi: Using Your Emotions as Fuel, and The Energy Waterfall are all revolutionary concepts that are both new and timeless, as well as accessible to all. I was in attendance the first time Caroline gave a keynote speech about The New Forgiveness. As she took to the podium and spoke; the power and presence of love filled the ballroom. The New Forgiveness was alive and moving into the hearts and minds of everyone young and old. Her husband and children were beaming beyond description. The banquet bartender was in tears, and it takes a lot to bring a bartender to tears!

I love this book. I love this woman. I love her husband. I love her children. I love her father. I love her mother. I love her sister. I love her niece. As you read The New Forgiveness you too will fall in love with Caroline Pena and her family.

The day that Caroline handed me the original manuscript for this book, she also gave me an Archangel Michael medallion. I carried that manuscript every day, everywhere I went for over nine months. I showed it and talked about it and read parts of it to everyone who would listen. I held the vision for this book because I know it has the power to transform generations of unforgiveness.

To this day I have never taken the Arch Angel Michael medallion off my neck. If you open your heart and let Caroline and The New Forgiveness in, your life, like mine, will never be the same. It takes and insurmountable amount of courage to realize one's vision. Caroline Pena has the courage of the classic hero and warrior. Apply the principles of The New Forgiveness, and you too will develop the courage to be the hero and warrior of your life, your dreams, and your visions.

Johnny Regan, Founder,
The Global Vision Conference

The New Forgiveness

ONE

Growing Up Is A Journey: Your Past Is Just A Lesson

How does your entire life lead up to your current mind set, create your beliefs, and serve as the building blocks to achieving the greatest happiness possible?

It's hard to conceive because we are all masters of forgetting small details that probably made a big impact on our future selves. My story you ask. I'm awakening my inner child especially for you, and solely in honor of you, for the greater good of all. I am sharing my story with you with a direct and streamlined focus to assist you with a masterful forgiving and healing process. I'm going far back in time now, into the long-lost memories stored in the sacred cave of my childhood, so that you may achieve an even deeper knowledge of the possibilities of the greatest gift you can give yourself, forgiveness.

The purpose of sharing my personal history and story is to help you embrace your past and begin to understand that we are

1

also but mere glimpses of our former selves. Understanding this allows you to be open to forgiving yourself and creates an even bigger opening for your embodiment of happiness in the present moment.

I was born and raised in Reynoldsburg, a suburb of Columbus, Ohio. My parents are still together to this day. There were successes and there were failures in my family, but I will tell you this, I had love and an abundance of food, shelter, and clothing. I had a roof over my head and many fun memories spending time with my parents and my big sister, Tammy. Tammy took me under her wings and protected me, all days always. Having an older sister, we were almost nine years apart, was a gift to me. She loved me from the moment I was born. I remember as a young girl feeling a sense of protection and safety and it was because of her. She made me feel safe like she was my safety net.

One sunny afternoon, I was ten years old, and I was riding my brand-new ten-speed bike, a gift from my parents for my tenth birthday. I loved that bike, so pink and shiny. It represented some freedom for me. I was riding back to my house and a neighborhood boy who was about my sister's age started throwing jellybeans at me. He threw them so hard it bruised my leg. Out of nowhere here comes my sister. She was raging down the road yelling at the kid until he retreated to his home and slammed the door. I can't remember what she said but I remember that he never bullied me again. Thanks, sis.

Graduating high school in 1997 I felt like I was a completely lost puppy in a jungle of trees where I felt that no matter where I looked, I could not find the horizon. Remember, we are going back in time here to when I was just eighteen years old. I couldn't feel happy or lustful for the future. I had no idea what lay ahead of me so I could only follow the advice and desires of others. I was not at all ready to suddenly be eighteen, considered an adult, and to be shipped off to college. I felt abandoned by my family, by life, by the world, by everyone. This isn't to say they did abandon me; I am saying that I felt that way. I had deep inner turmoil that, most likely, was well hidden to the outside world.

My parents drove me from my childhood home in Reynoldsburg, Ohio to Kent State University after the summer of 1997. I was terrified. I remember crying when they dropped me off and trying to run after the car as they pulled away. It was a sad and lonely day for me; I don't know why I wasn't elated and excited like so many other new students that were itching for their first day of college. I will never know why I struggled so much to fit in and just feel happy. The only thing I can say is that I always felt that there was so much more to my human existence than what I was currently experiencing. I felt a ball of fire, deep inside of me even as a little girl. I just didn't have the self-power, knowledge, confidence or guidance I needed at the time, so I defined my emotions and lack of understanding life as a personal defect.

I always had trouble feeling that I fit in and going off to a new school did not change that for me. I was alone in a sea of faces with no real solid goal and no definitive dream or vision for my life. I was just a ball of stagnant self-doubt and depression, and because of that I gained thirty pounds and almost lost myself completely. About halfway through the year I was moved to a different dormitory, and I knocked on the door of a girl who needed a roommate. I felt I was not likable or lovable and I was so shy. The door opened and I was greeted with a smile. Her name was Regina and she has been my best friend now for over twenty years.

Regina was one of the first lights of true friendship in my life. She accepted me and loved me as a friend long before I was able to be as kind to her in return. She waited with love as I trampled through messed up relationships, terrible decision-making skills, and hour-long depressed conversations. She was a gift of love and light to me and has been every day since the day we met. We both left Kent State that year. She went back to her hometown, and I went back to the Columbus area. I had flunked out of school. Between 1998 and 2000 I tried to go back to school, and I enrolled at Columbus State University for a short time. I got a roommate and my own apartment; things were looking up. My roommate and I were very close; he was a good man. We both got jobs at a local non-profit and would party together on the weekends. He drank a lot, and I always worried about his health.

To this day I cannot recall why we had a falling out, but we did, and we parted ways. I always loved him as a good friend, and when I tell you I cannot recall to this day what we argued over, I truly cannot remember. What I do remember is him asking to meet me at a bar to talk one day. I met him. He was so sad as he held my hand over the table and begged me to move back in and be his roommate again. I had moved on by that time and looking back it is a pivotal moment where I wish I would have been there for him more as a friend.

Around the end of 2000 things went even more downhill for me. My parents were amid moving out of my childhood home, which was my foundation of comfort and safety. I felt lost, without a home, a family, a future, and then one day I just quit. I quit everything. I quit school. I quit my job. I quit my connections with people. I quit my entire life and I drove. I took all the money I had in the bank, $2000, and my old beat up Camry; I took everything I could fit in my car and left the rest behind at a dumpster. I drove south. Good riddance, Ohio. With my middle finger in the air I refused to look behind me as I kept driving.

My destination was Fort Lauderdale, Florida. Beautiful, sunny Florida where I always remembered the sun was shining and the beach waves were crashing. As a little girl, who had visited many times in the past, I knew I just had to get to where the sun was always shining. I needed to be bright, feel bright, and change, well, everything. I drove all the way from Columbus, Ohio to Savannah, Georgia without stopping. Pulling off at an exit I got a room at a Days Inn to rest. It was nighttime when I got to the room. I was just twenty-one years old. I sat on a bed, halfway from where I was running from, and halfway to the sun I was running toward. Too prideful to turn back and too scared to move forward I froze. In utter loneliness, I rolled up in a tight ball, and cried until I was like a wilted-up raisin and eventually fell asleep.

The next morning, I dragged myself to the car. I started the engine and for the first time I looked back. Which way to turn? I just stared at the sky which was both sunny and overcast that day. Then I felt what I would describe as a knowing. It wasn't like a voice you could hear audibly but a voice nonetheless. It felt like a magnet pulling me south, so towards the sun I went.

I pressed the gas pedal and found myself on the freeway continuing south. I was saving myself but I was also leaving some people behind. I spent years in wonderment as to why or how this all happened, always thinking about the way it did, but I do forgive myself. My personal burdens had become so heavy that I needed a sudden jolt into a new reality. In the long run, those I left behind either moved on without me or to this day have enjoyed many visits to my home in Florida. They are now so happy for me that I have since found peace, experienced joy and have a grateful heart. It wasn't an easy road back then, but I did make it to Florida.

I had a wonderful aunt and uncle who did their best to be there for me but I was not their child and it was hard for them. I had many jobs, many small crummy apartments, and many terrible relationships and even got taken advantage of by a youth pastor at a church I was attending. I was vulnerable, lost, extremely lonely and needed to feel safe. He made me feel like he was my boy-   friend and fed on my vulnerabilities.

I never realized, until twenty years later through the process of writing this book, how much some of the things that happened in the past really affected me. I told you, we tend to forget the small details, or even the big details if they are far enough behind us. I am not sure I will ever truly understand why I never felt that I fit in as a child and a young adult, but I don't really need to understand. I have let the past go. Who I was then, as well as all my inner personal struggles, brought me to where I am today. You see, those experiences eventually compelled me to move to another state. Every experience was there to serve me.

The journey that brought me to Florida was showered with the many different relationships, jobs, feelings of abandonment and friendships all bottled up into one significant moment where I got into my car and drove, by myself, five states away, with no plan, and never ever looked back. If we are willing to admit it, some of us may be willing to recognize that we are masters of finding a beautiful little cave inside of us to hide our past, an action we believe is the pathway to achieving what we think is a current state of happiness. This method however, is what leads to depression and unrest as well as a lack of physical wellness. It makes us think that life as we know it is "as good as it gets."

I didn't realize until now how past events impacted me and took part in shaping the exact person I am today. I was very vulnerable arriving in Fort Lauderdale alone, young, and emotionally lost. At the time, there were some nights that I prayed not to wake up at all. The only time I felt I was not alone was once per week when I would sit in a pew alone in a church full of hundreds of people. I would sit there and try to weave myself into their lives, somehow trying to make myself important to those around me. I was invisible. I would dread the end of each service when all the families dispersed happily, and I had to go back to my studio apartment alone. From that moment, I would be waiting another seven days to be a part of a room full of people once again.

The youth pastor was charming and well liked, and I had a crush on him. I didn't fit in. I wasn't young enough to be one of the children in the youth group, but I wasn't old enough, or mature enough, to be a leader. So there I was, somewhere in between. You guessed it, he started dating me. We weren't really boyfriend and girlfriend, but we were dating enough that we were intimate.

I went on a youth group trip with him; I yearned for his attention so badly I would do anything for it. We were intimate during that weekend trip, and he whispered in my ear that it was every pastor's dream. In the end we never ended up being together and I was left even lonelier than before.

He never really wanted much to do with me except for the casual weekend excursions where we would travel together. He made me feel special and then he dropped me. I've always felt taken advantage of by him. I always felt, even though I was old enough to give consent to the relationship, that he did take advantage of my vulnerability and loneliness. As the years have gone by in my life I've realized how cruel and unusual it was for him to treat me that way; he knew I was weak. He was in a position of power and authority, and he used that to take advantage of me.

Each one of us has a unique and ever-changing story to tell. It's beautiful at times and it's messy. It's embarrassing and full of self-judgment. Our stories can be hard to tell, as fear can often override the necessity to be honest about your story, if being honest is even just to yourself. I want you to know that you are not alone. Everyone may not tell the muddied and embarrassing parts of their lives out loud, but we all have them.

One Sunday evening after church, after the sun set, and the darkness had set in, I just lay flat on the cold tile floor and I gave up. I did not want to live anymore. I didn't know it then but looking back now I know was suicidal. I had no desire to live and just wanted my life to end, so I begged God to make me fall asleep and never wake up. I had lost hope and cried for hours. What happened next is my first memory of starting to really believe in angels and those that watch over us. I had hit rock-bottom, but from the bottom, I found my first sense of self-love and peace. I had crashed hard to the bottom of the **"Energy Waterfall."** I will go into detail about how emotions progress and power your "Energy Waterfall" in Chapter Eight.

From rock bottom, I suddenly found a sense of peace, a place of calm and an understanding within my spirit. It was then I began to know the love of God. I had a feeling that I had never ever experienced before. I stood up and I had my second "knowing" experience, it was like an inner voice that said, "You can be happy, you are loved, you can start by loving yourself." We all have those dark moments that we may even forget over time, like my youth pastor story. It was so very long ago that it no longer affects me.

Time has allowed me to see my role in that play, time has allowed me to mature, to understand better how people and relationships work, or don't work. It's a piece to my life puzzle. Now that I see how important every story in my life is, to leading me where I am today, I can say that I am thankful for that time, and the way I was treated.

When you see things through a slightly different lens, it gives you the fortitude to achieve forgiveness.

This was the beginning of an awakening for me, although I didn't know it at the time. Years later as a licensed holistic physician I always drew from this experience. When a new patient would come in I could instantly see if they had given up hope of getting better. I learned with these patients to always say the words, "You can get better, it starts with hope. Hope is the foundation to healing, and today we restore that hope."

You don't know what someone is going through when you cross paths with them. You don't know the many thousands of pieces to their complicated life puzzle. Be nice. It's hard sometimes but be nice. I find when people are being unkind that it usually means they're feeling very sad or suffering in some way. I came to this conclusion because if I'm honest, if I'm ever in a bad mood in public, or feel that I came across unkind, it's always because I'm currently going through something very difficult. Self-reflection is good; it helps you understand other people and it helps you to be more forgiving more often.

I chose an extremely hard path when I left Ohio with no plan and only $2000 to my name. That same year I received a call from an old and dear friend of mine, whom I have always called, "The Countess" and she always called me "Monchhichi." I miss her. She said she was sorry to tell me that my beloved roommate had been drinking and driving and was killed in a car accident. I hadn't spoken to him for over a year or so and I so badly wanted a chance to tell him how much he meant to me as a friend.

I flew up to Ohio for the funeral. Pictures of the two of us were plastered all over the room. I realized how special our friendship was to him and to his family. It was sad and it hit me hard as the sadness set in. To this day I miss him but I have a peace within myself, in knowing that my time here on earth with him was meaningful and loving. I think of him fondly, always.

After he died, I was asked to move in with this very new boyfriend of mine. So, I picked up and moved from Fort Lauderdale to northern Florida, again lacking much of a plan. He ended up hitting me and verbally abusing me. One evening he was whisked off to jail from a call I made half-naked outside of his house. The bruises on my face told the story. The police officer told me he could hold him for only two days and handed me a pamphlet. I looked down and saw that it was a pamphlet for battered women. My brain almost exploded! "I am not an abused woman!" It outright pissed me off. But he was right, at that moment, I was being abused.

So, there I was again. As the police car drove away I looked at the house, my still beat up Camry, my beat up face, my two cats, and all my belongings and said, "Well, I have two days, which direction do I go?" Early the next morning I had a hitch put on my car and rented a tiny pull-behind U-Haul. I stuffed all I could call mine in that U-Haul, along with my two cats in the car, left the rest behind and started driving. Yep, back up north to Ohio. Where else could a lost puppy go? Defeated, with my tail between my legs, I drove back north to where my life first began.

The next two years were better. I enrolled at The Ohio State University and was determined to graduate with straight A's and with honors. I got a full-time job as a nanny and took fifteen to twenty credit hours each semester. I prevailed! I graduated with honors and with my past college failures finally behind me. I paid all my school bills and rent on my own. I had some money, a bachelor's degree and finally, some pride.

I missed the sun. The magnet was back, so in September of 2004 I drove back to Florida. This time I had a plan. I had a full-time job already lined up working as a youth recreation director for a local nonprofit. I had a nice apartment lined up and a brand new 2004 Saturn Ion. I was very proud of myself. I did have two complete nervous breakdowns before graduation in 2004. I don't want you to think it was a breeze. Having a full-time job, full-time school, full-time homework, and full-time obsession with having perfect grades just about took me under. But I kept paddling, sometimes just above water, and I didn't drown. It did take me seven years to achieve a four-year bachelor's, but, hey, I did it.

Over the next few years, I switched careers to a licensed community association manager, then to a retail store owner, and eventually to a holistic practice manager and yoga teacher. I realized I had the spirit of an entrepreneur. I just had to continue to create new things, new jobs, and new beginnings. I wanted to evolve and grow. I started to allow myself to follow my heart and dreams and not the dreams and expectations that others had for me.

Use extreme caution if you're trying to live up to someone else's standards for you. You may be cutting yourself short. The dreams you have for yourself may well exceed their expectations.

Do what brings you peace. Read that again. Do what brings you peace. Do what you love, what you want, and what you need to have a truly happy life. Follow the joy in your heart and the money and prosperity will follow. The happier you are, the better off not only you will be, but the people and the world around you will reflect your joy as well.

When you put too much stock into what others want from you, or into what you believe will help you fit in or be accepted, you lead yourself down a path of misery, and here's why. Whatever you choose to do in your life there will always be someone who agrees with it and someone who does not. If you choose to do what pleases others you may achieve pleasing them but there will inevitably be someone who disagrees. The same circumstance holds true when you follow your heart, your dreams, and your desires. There will be people who are disappointed and those who will rejoice. There's only one main difference in the two circumstances and that's whether you're happy or not. You can live by listening to your heart or you can ignore your true calling and try to please others. Do you see the difference? There's just one -you; how you feel, that's the only difference. The main difference between the two is that in one of them you are at peace, you are healthy and happy. In the other, someone may be proud of you, but you are miserable. You do you and the rest will fall quite nicely into place.

TWO

The Beginning Of Peace: When Losing It All Is All Part Of The Plan

I had opened a retail store in 2005 thinking I would revel in my success. Just one short year after opening my doors the market crash of 2006 happened and my store completely tanked. I lost my entire business, my family member's investment money, my house was forced into foreclosure, and I was bankrupt. I spent six months sitting on my couch in a home the bank was taking from under me. I watched Miami Heat play basketball and ate chicken wings for months, engulfed by an overwhelming sense of failure.

I had no job, little money, no home and was once again looking for a direction. Then one day I started taking meditation classes called Raja Yoga. I did the mediations daily. I focused intently on happiness and cracked my brain into a new way of thinking. Thank you, Bhavna Ben; you have left this world now but your presence as a Raja Yoga healer snapped me out of it. You relit my inner flame and my gratitude for your teachings are forever immense and eternal.

Remember that $2000 dollars I had when I first made my journey to Florida? Yep, that's the exact same amount of money I now had to my name after losing it all. I looked up local yoga schools and enrolled. What did I have to lose? I gave them almost all my money and graduated as a registered yoga teacher and I was back. I started teaching all private yoga classes in clients' homes. The referrals came quickly, and I made very good money. I was also offered a part-time job as manager of a holistic practice and started looking for a new home.

Little did I know my entire life path was about to change in a very big way, forever. I was asked to attend an invitation only Halloween party in October of 2010 and ended up meeting the man who would eventually become my husband. It was kismet really. He was dressed as Julius Caesar and I was dressed as Cleopatra. We have a picture of the moment we met and I just love that about my life story. We dated for a short period of time. It only took a few dates for us both to fully realize that we were meant for each other, we were meant to be, and we loved each other. We hadn't said it yet but we both knew it.

It was the first time in my life that I was not alone. Not only that, the soul, body and mind connection I had with him allowed me to know that he would never fail me and that I would not be left alone. I was fully loved. One afternoon he sent a text message to me, some beautiful poetry from his heart. He said, "My love for you is the bond that keeps my mind, being, spirit and matter altogether. Without it, I would be scattered in pieces."

Three months after we met, I found out I was pregnant. We were barely boyfriend and girlfriend and had only known each other for a short period of time so how could he respond? How would he respond? I invited him over to my house for dinner. I cooked, we embraced, and we enjoyed the evening. I had something to tell him,   something big and life changing.

I sat on the couch. The sun had set, and now with our stomachs full we could relax. I sat to his left with my right knee on the couch facing him. I looked at him and I said, "I have something to tell you." He stared at me. I said, "Well… (pause…) I am pregnant." Then I said, "And the baby is yours." He said, "Oh." I sat silently. He processed the information. I was thirty-two at the time and he was forty-two. He was recently divorced and had just gotten a break from some of the obligations of a family life, so how would he respond? Who would blame him for any kind of response, I mean honestly?

About a minute went by and this is exactly what he said - word for word. I will never forget the all-encompassing and embracing energy of his reply. He said, "Well, first of all I want you to know that you are not alone," (pause) He continued. "I will always be here for you and for the baby. I will take care of you and you don't have to worry about anything, okay?" We hugged in silence for a while.

I wish I could tell you about a beautiful birth story but, as you will soon find out, it was just the beginning of a fight we never could have imagined. We found out at twenty weeks gestation that our little baby boy, peacefully embraced in the warmth and love of my womb, was developing with his intestines and stomach outside of his body just floating around in the amniotic fluid. We would be fighting for his life. Would he survive? It was our obvious first question.

THREE

Maddox

The journey to understanding forgiveness has been a long one for me. Navigating through life has been the greatest joy and the most challenging struggle. As the years of my life have passed by, I've come to realize the ultimate complexity of it. There is always so much more to learn. Only now do I fully understand how our experiences, and how the relationship we have to the emotions we store in response to those experiences, play the biggest role in creating our personal realities. Once you fully understand how your experiences, your reactions, and the emotions they create are just energy, you can turn emotional pain into the fuel you need to heal your hurt and create a moment that propels you to forgiveness and to moving forward in life.

One of the biggest struggles of my life was also the beginning of my journey to achieving forgiveness. It was the start to a long learning process, eventually leading to mastering a way to forgiving myself and others. Little did I know that this achievement, once learned and practiced, would be applied continually in my life as new hurtful circumstances would come my way.

I was thirty-two weeks pregnant when the journey began. One evening I was sitting at home with my boyfriend, Cesar. We had just enjoyed a fun and relaxing day together. It was evening now, and time to relax as we both sent love to the baby boy growing inside of me. We had found out early in the pregnancy that our baby had a challenging condition. He suffered from Gastroschisis, a condition where he was going to be born with his intestines and stomach on the outside of his body.

We were watching some television when I said, "You know, it's kind of funny, I haven't felt him kick all day but I'm sure everything's fine." Cesar didn't agree, and he rushed me to the hospital. They monitored me and found out that there was a total lack of fetal movement. It was like my baby was sleeping but for way too long. I didn't leave the hospital that night. Two weeks later, after being on bed rest, they rushed me into the operating room. They told me that we were going in for an emergency C-section because something was happening with my baby.

Not knowing what would happen was the hardest part of the doctors rushing into the room. I was terrified and it was torturous for me. Weeks before I had made Cesar make a promise to me. I made him promise that if I went in for a C-section that they would let me kiss my baby's face before they whisked him off to the Neo-natal Intensive Care Unit.

They took my baby, who we named Maddox, out of my womb and wrapped him up with every single inch of his intestines and stomach on the outside of his body. Thanks to Cesar I was able to kiss his face. I wasn't sure what was going to happen but to be honest I never once thought that he wouldn't make it. My breast milk came in a few hours later and by the next morning I was so engorged and in so much pain that I was screaming for my baby. My body ached to be with my son, skin to skin, to care for him, but I couldn't breast-feed my child or even touch him.

I started pumping my breastmilk and was able to fill up a five cubic foot freezer full of milk within weeks. I wouldn't leave his bedside and I begged them not to discharge me. They did have to eventually, but I sat there in a chair next to him for hours and hours and hours, day after day, week after week, until I finally fell asleep sitting up. I refused to leave Maddox's bedside. I knew I had rights to be there. I knew that they could not keep me out, so there I stayed.

One day a nurse came up to me and said, "You look exhausted, you need to sleep." I told her to either roll up a bed next to my child or stop telling me I looked tired because I was not leaving him, and I meant it. I know she was being nice but believe me when I tell you that the most dangerous place on this planet is between a mother and her child. When your child is in pain there is one focus and one feeling only - protect your child at all costs.

Nothing in my life could have prepared me for the intense connection I would have with my baby. I was now a mother. That's a bond you could never find words to describe. I had a silver cord directly from my son to me, a strong bond, one that would prove to be important in the following months of nurturing him back to health. I was now his watcher and I watched over him diligently, never taking my sight off the one and only end goal, his health.

Two months had now gone by as he continued to struggle through multiple infections and growth delays. In the months he spent in the NICU, he almost went into cardiac arrest when his carotid artery PICC line leaked fluids around his heart. He endured numerous infections and setbacks, the worst of which was a Chylothorax, a leaking of fluid around the lungs, between the lung and chest wall. It's like being suffocated, and it's extremely painful. By the time he was two months old he was only topping off the scale at just around six pounds, but this was great progress.

A few weeks after our boy was born I found out that there was a place called the Quantum House on the hospital campus. Thankfully one of the nurses had compassion for me and I ended up getting a room there because of her. I was able to stay on the grounds of the hospital while my son was fighting for his life. Day in and day out I was able to be right at my baby's bedside. A newborn, especially one who's sick, needs their mother. Having a room at the Quantum House allowed me to rest. I could at least go back to a bed that was only a four-minute golf cart ride away from my baby boy's bedside. I could sleep. I could pump my breastmilk. Anytime I had to be near my baby boy I could call one of the guards and they would pick me up and take me quickly to my son.

Cesar called me one evening, probably around six o'clock or so. The sun had already set. He was keeping up a full-time job while all of this was going on. He had to think of so many people, as well as continue to make money and hold a job. Moreover, he was also worrying about his newborn son's life. But this night, I specifically told him not to come and see me. I didn't want to see him, the father of our baby boy. I was in a very dark place. It's like being in a dark room in a deep pit. There are no windows, no doors, no light, just darkness. I knew I loved him but I also knew I needed to be alone.

I was kind to him on the phone. I said, "It's ok. It's not you my love, I just need to be alone, and I don't want to see you." Sometimes self-pity just gets the best of us. I think that is what was happening to me that night, I was so sad that I just wanted to feel sadder. In a way, I think it made me feel like I was doing something to help my baby boy heal faster. I guess I thought that my continued suffering would somehow help baby Maddox to know we were in this together and that he was not alone.

Somewhere, somehow in the midst of all this, this man refused to leave me trapped in the dark forest alone, and refused to believe my words. He showed up to my door while I was lost in worry for the life of my child. Sadly, I had not been able to see his suffering too. He loved me so much and I knew that. His love for me and his son was palpable. He did everything he could to help our son and to help me survive the fear and sadness that had engulfed me. Like I said, I begged him not to come that night, but he loved me so much that somehow he knew he had to. It was late and there was a knock at the door. I wanted to be alone and spend the evening laying on the floor, being in the presence of God, and crying my eyes out. I thought there was a need to constantly beg and plead for my baby's life.

I opened the door and I wanted to spend time being angry that he didn't listen to me. I wanted to be angry that he came when I told him that I needed space to myself and that I needed time. But as soon as I opened the door I felt nothing but love and light again. That was palpable for both of us. He hugged me and I embraced him back. I was finally able to feel his suffering and so for the first time, we cried together, bonded at that moment by one emotion, love. He's always been a spot of inspiration for me. He doesn't stay in negativity too long. It's largely because of him that we all survived that time in our baby's life. He did his best, and his best at times, was far better than mine. For this, I am eternally grateful to him.

Over the months I had not gone to my home which was about an hour from the hospital. One day I decided to take a day trip there to reconnect with the house and gather some items. I went home and sat on the couch. I remember the sun was shining and there were people around trying to comfort me, though their own faces were sad too. I started crying because I was disconnected from my son. I was too far away from the other part of me. I had to go back. Putting so many miles between my baby and me only triggered greater sadness.

I started driving back to the hospital and I had come to my darkest of days. I don't know how I knew to reach out to her, or what made me feel comfortable enough being so vulnerable to make a phone call, but I imagine it was because I was feeling so completely dark and I had nothing to lose by showing the suffering of my motherly soul. I had a connection with her because she was the first person who knew that I was pregnant. She had become a friend, like a motherly spirit. I trusted her. Her name was Leigh Anne, and she is to this day an angel on earth, my dear sweet friend.

As I drove I called her and made a plea for help. I felt like I was suddenly faced with picking up an old metal rusty payphone in the dark vastness of hell, and had one phone call that just might reach the outside world. It was like I was going to call out but no one would hear me, not my angels, nobody, just a complete isolation of my soul. I dialed. Then, out of nowhere, in the darkness, a voice reached out and grabbed my hand. She answered, "Hello." I said, "I am not OK." These were my exact words.

Thank God she answered that day. I will never forget the bluntest of the three words I spoke or the powerful energy behind them. I continued, "I'm on my way to the NICU to see my son and I am very depressed. I'm beyond sadness and I don't even feel pain anymore. I feel hopeless." She lived about an hour away from the hospital. I was probably only twenty minutes away at the time I had called her.

To this day I don't know how she did it but she arrived at the hospital before I even got there. I had parked my car and walked into the NICU. I saw the friendly face of a woman who was always there to give out hugs and welcome parents of sick babies at the front desk. I'll never forget her. I said hello to her and as I turned to enter the NICU, I saw my sweet friend Leigh Anne sitting there waiting for me. She didn't say the words, "I will help carry you," as I walked toward her, but I heard a whisper in my mind and I knew it was her telling me exactly that. Sometimes we need to be carried, and we need a friend. We cannot suffer great tragedies alone. We are not meant to, and when a friend reaches out to help carry you say, "Yes."

I sat down next to her. My shoulders were low and my energy was low. I'm sure I had a sallow looking complexion and it felt as if the whites of my eyes were a gray hue. I just felt gray all over, through and through. She came to pull me out of the darkness that day; it wasn't instantaneous, but she pulled me out. Where there was no window before, there was now a window of light. I was still in a dark place but I saw the light. She lifted me up from the pit of darkness and showed me that everything was going to be okay and I believed her. It wasn't just because I wanted to believe her, it was because I knew that my son was going to survive. I could feel it. I knew I was going to survive too. She saved me from myself that day just by showing up and being a light. I don't know what would've happened if she had not come. Angels come in many ways, and in many forms, but that day, this angel came in human form. Her name was Leigh Anne and she hugged me until I started to feel whole again.

I didn't know it then, but looking back on this experience in 2011, it was the beginning of my understanding of energy and how it works on our emotions. My son did come home. He was born four pounds, five ounces in August of 2011. By the end of October 2011, he was two months old and weighing in at about six pounds. He was tiny but he was mighty. After weeks of being tied down to his back, with his stomach and intestines hanging in a silo above him, allowing gravity to slowly make space in his abdominal cavity to hold his organs, he endured surgery and had all his parts successfully sewn back into place. In the end he survived it, all of it!

The day we brought our baby Maddox home was the most exciting and terrifying day of our lives. I had never been without a team of nurses around me and my son, monitoring and watching over every beat of his tiny little heart. We pulled into the driveway of our home, with his baby room waiting to embrace him, so beautifully and heartily decorated for his arrival. It was a day I had focused on with extreme intent every second since the moment of his birth. I only saw this moment as he fought for his life, and for his freedom from the four plastic walls of his incubator. I can only imagine what he must have been feeling as the fresh air and gentle breeze brushed against his baby cheek, as he felt the free world for the first time since leaving the comfort of my womb.

He had a crib - a wonderful, warm and cozy crib… which he almost never slept in. He had a long way to go to embodying his internal strength, but he was home, and he survived. We put a mattress on the floor of his room. Either Cesar or I slept there, with him by our side, for almost a year. He grew, he thrived, and day by day, he continues to grow up a hearty, healthy and vivacious human being.

Embrace of Love

I love you my child
Earth angel of my dreams
A gift from the heavens
What does this love mean?

I was a vessel, you traveled far
You came through me, and here you are

When I see you
When I look at your face
When I hold you and hug you
When we embrace

I feel I am flying
Wrapped around, my wings
I am your angel
Here on earth, for all things

On this earth
Or in heaven above
Always with you my child
With infinite Love

"Caroline Pena"

The New Forgiveness

FOUR

The Catalyst to Change

Most of us have a trauma experience to tell. We have one or more specific instances that we go to in our minds when we are dealing with our emotional pain - we have a defining moment in our life. There's something major that affected us so deeply that it changed our life, or the way we view life, forever. Those moments are the ones where we can ravel in the self-pity of it, or we can fly over and soar above it with new wisdom, overcoming even the most heinous of times.

"Sometimes we think there's no way we can live with or find peace after something that has happened, but we can. If you don't believe that, then the darker forces have you right where they want you."

The worst of our experiences are almost always, eventually, the catalyst to change in our lives. Have there been circumstances in your life that happened to you, possibly causing you so much resentment, hatred and fear, that it just about killed your soul, shattering your belief in peace or the possibility of living a happy day to day life? If not, you are lucky, and I am so happy for you. More than likely though, since you are reading this book, you have something or someone to forgive, and you do have hatred that needs to be healed.

In my past, I endured a home invasion that was done by someone known by the family. The resentment that the experience created in my heart, and the lack of support and understanding I received, just about ruined my marriage and my sense of self-love and inner peace. The deep pain I experienced was two-fold. First, was the pain of the trauma from the experience, and second, was not being able to understand why others couldn't see it through my eyes, through my lens, and feel exactly how I felt. Forgiveness was up to me and I was failing miserably.

Before I tell you this story, I want to tell you that there is a huge sense of freedom that comes from exposing the most vulnerable chapters of my life story. It's freeing for me, and telling our stories can help heal other people, not just ourselves. When we hear the life stories of others it makes us feel that we are not alone and that healing is possible. It is because of this that I am sharing my story with you. From my heart, my deepest desire is for you to heal too, as I have.

On an even more personal note, I have told this story hundreds of times since it happened. Yes, literally hundreds of times. I always told the story looking for the listener to be as mad and as hurt as I was. It wasn't the response I got. People felt bad for me but they just couldn't feel my excruciating pain. They didn't stare in the face of darkness. They couldn't understand it because, in the end, it didn't happen to them, it happened to me. They were not there.

My son was just a few months old when I was put to the ultimate test. He was very little, and although he was a few months old, he was still healing from his difficult start to life and being hospitalized for months before his homecoming. He was playing catch up from being born premature and gaining back his health from being born so sick. I was home alone, just me and my little baby Maddox. The sun was shining. It was early and I was in the kitchen starting my day. My son was in the family room adjacent to the kitchen. I could see him clearly. He was so happy and vibrant in his little rocker. We were smiling at each other as I mashed up some cooked apples, and I was still basking in his successful homecoming.

Suddenly I heard some movement by my front door, then again, footsteps. My heart started racing as I knew someone was in the house. I ran toward my baby to grab him; the plan was to get to the back sliding glass doors and run. As I went to get my baby I saw the edge of a foot going up the stairs. I turned to run, looking back for a moment, I saw a police officer standing inside of my house blocking my front door. I screamed in terror - he was a huge man, powerful and tall. He demanded I come to him. As I walked forward I saw someone else going up the stairs.

This beastly police officer pushed me up against the wall. I could smell his breath as I cringed and held tightly to my baby boy. He put his finger on my nose and said, "I know women like you. You will stand here, and you will not move while he takes what he wants to. If you move, I will have your baby taken from you." I cried and froze as I looked at the man going up the stairs. He had pure joy on his face. A look of total hatred, or worse, a look of someone who lacked all love; it was like staring into a void. This person was a close family relationship to me and had some access to the house which was how he was able to get in and convince the police that he had rights there. He did not, but it was obviously unclear to the officer.

I stared into the face of darkness that day and it terrified me. It shook me and I felt like I was losing a battle or being taken out of this world. It was a look that would plaster in my cells like a snapshot photo, and this photo would recall for me with the post-traumatic stress disorder I had for the years to come. The feeling of the loss of control, no longer feeling safe in my own home, and his hatred for me, filled me with resentment and fear. It was awful. That day the darkness won.

In the time that followed, I could never leave a door unlocked again, or a garage or sliding glass door open, even to let in the fresh air. I couldn't hear a knock at the door without having a panic attack. If a branch would brush up against the house my sense of safety fell off quickly as I would struggle to catch my breath. For years, no matter how deeply I inhaled, I could not expand my lungs widely enough to feel as if I was receiving a good cleansing breath.

I reached out to some lawyers at the time. The police officer was wrong. He had no right to enter my home, nor did the man, but no lawyer was willing to take on the police department. I had no recourse, no support, and very little sympathy coming my way.

The loneliness was the least of the emotions that overwhelmed me, but that settled in too, once I realized that I was the only warrior for my son's safety and for myself that day.

Many years have gone by since then and I have finally let go of the story. What I mean by this is that I have made a conscious decision to feel better, to move forward, and to heal. I no longer have a need for someone else to agree with me, feel how I felt, or even to sympathize. It was my journey alone. I also know something now that I never understood before. I realize now that I stared into the face of darkness that day, and he was not entirely himself when he invaded my home. The only battle weapon darkness has on any person of light is fear. It was his body and sense of entitlement that dragged him into the house, but there was a darkness that had taken over him too.

I was weak and wounded at the time, still healing from the trauma of fighting for my son's life, so when I looked right into his eyes, I saw worse than hatred for me. I saw a void and a complete lack of love. Fear settled easily into my vulnerable heart. As I said darkness won the battle that day; I was afraid, and it worked. I was weak from months of fighting for my son's life, so it was the perfect environment for darker forces to finesse their way into my heart and soul. The darkness was feeding on that man's own vulnerabilities and fears at the time too. It was indeed a perfect storm. Now I can tell the story so others can see where I am now, understand how I have healed, and begin to believe fully that forgiveness is possible. How did I achieve forgiveness? Oh, dear one, let this journey begin.

The tear-soaked rug in my closet saw many days of sadness and anger with me in the years that followed the home invasion. I would retreat into that space, behind a locked bathroom door, and closed bi-fold glass mirrors, and bawl my eyeballs out until I was sure there couldn't be a single moist drop left in me. Then I would cry some more. I would roll up into an even tighter ball, and I would stare into the threads of the rug begging for a release of this resentment. Hatred had a hold on me. The hardest part of my life was constantly pressing at me, like a voice in my ears, "Forgive him for the invasion, let it go Caroline."

> *"Over and over again, day after day, month after month, year after year, my mind told me to let the hatred go, but my soul's righteous grasp on the injustice of it had a tighter hold on me."*

I would think to myself, how is letting it go right? If I forgive him, how does it NOT mean that I am saying what happened was ok? If I let him back into my life is that a defeat on my part? Does forgiveness require reconciliation? How do I keep myself safe from him invading me or my safe space ever again?

Over time I began to realize that hatred, resentment, and worst of all, the inability and unwillingness to forgive was like an addiction. Hatred can have a hold on you until you decide at the core of who you are that you are ready to quit, that you will quit, and that you are ready to let it go.

> *"On absolutely every single journey to a healed heart and a happy life, you will eventually be faced with the hardest thing to overcome - yourself."*

Once you've read the books, done the meditations, gone on the retreats, whatever it takes to get to a place where the post-traumatic stress doesn't rule your life, you are finally left with yourself. What will you do? In that moment of darkness meeting light, will you rise up and let it go, or will you retreat to the closet once again to cry tears of injustice?

For years I chose the closet, I chose tears. I chose to be right; I chose to tell my story. I was right, it was horrible what happened to me. It was inconceivable to think that I could ever allow him into my life in any way again, right? Well, sometimes things aren't that simple.

There are other people in your life that make up your tribe. Your relationships are intertwined, in a divine way, there to serve you, challenge you, and bring you to embody your greatest and highest version of yourself.

I realized over time that my desire to triumph over my own broken heart would eventually be the energy that would transform my tears into forgiveness. Every tear that flowed from my eyes was also all the love I had for myself and my family. Every tear was like a retreat into the warm comfort of the center of my heart. Every tear wrapped me with love. There were millions of tears, over what felt like millions of years, just rolling over my body, patiently waiting for me to wake up into forgiveness and transform into joy.

For the months and years that followed I did the self-work to heal. I read dozens of books on forgiveness. I listened to audio books as I drove. I did forgiveness journals. I even prayed on the floor, begging for some kind of pill that would rip the hatred out of my heart. Nothing worked and I did not feel any better. The framework of the all the books on forgiveness were the same. The workshops were the same. Just let it go. Forgive because your religion tells you to. Forgiveness is for you not them. It never resonated with me and it never worked. I didn't understand the message. I didn't feel better, and I was willing to say to myself, there has to be a way, there just has to be a way to heal.

I am not saying that those other approaches to forgiveness cannot work. I know they can and have for many. I also know that if it never worked for me, never really lead me to true forgiveness, then I wasn't the only one who needed a new way to achieve a healed heart. To start I needed to understand what "forgiveness" really truly was.

The New Forgiveness

FIVE

Experiences: They are There to Serve You Intro to The New Forgiveness Method

Our human experience and the way we live our life here on this earth is twisted and wonderful, horrible, and magnificent, full of joy and fear, sometimes all at the same time. Not even one of us gets to have a life journey that is void of any feeling that we consider to be less than joy. We all must endure injustices and hardships. Everything you've ever learned, ever been through, or anything that has caused you to have a complete and utter shutdown or breakdown in your life is there to serve you. You've learned from these experiences, you've grown, morphed, changed, evolved, become wiser, and had opportunities to make new maybe even better decisions, haven't you?

Look at my past. I endured a terrifying home invasion right after birthing a sick baby fighting for his life, now home and embracing his health. These experiences changed me forever. I'm a better person for it actually. When you can learn not only to survive, but learn to thrive, you've mastered love. When you have love for yourself, love for your experiences, and especially love for those that hurt you the most, it becomes extremely hard for depression to take over you ever again, at least not for too long. You get better at dealing with hardships faster. You become a master of letting go, through repetition and practice and achieve forgiveness.

The experiences we have are a part of our life story and are there to make you stronger. You can decide whether to dwell on the heartache of the experience or you can decide to embody gratitude for overcoming the worst, and for being able to see the best. Cesar and I were lucky to have the birth experience we had with our baby boy. We fought as a family unit together. We fought together, me, Cesar and baby Maddox, and we won. I would never trade the growth, internal strength and personal love of life that I gained from that experience. To this day, every time I look at my son, I have so much gratitude for the fact that I can look at him and embrace him. I get to be his mother and I get to help him grow into manhood. This is a blessing I may not be able to truly see or appreciate without the experience we had as a family.

I stayed home with him for the first year and a half after his homecoming. It's one of the top most treasured times in my life. The memories I have of embodying and being fully in my motherly spirit, and completely focused on another human being, filled me with so much hope for the souls of the world. I realized that I am never alone, and that we, as a human race, are never alone. Most of my childhood I felt alone. It wasn't that I had any lack of love, on the contrary, I had a lot of love; I had a loving family and many blessings. But deep inside, I always felt alone; I couldn't explain it, I just did. I think God has a way of showing us what we cannot easily see by gifting us these experiences. It took meeting a good man, and a terrifying birth story, for me to learn that I was not alone, and never was.

What we all do individually, and collectively, affects the web of people with whom we share this earth. Every relationship, interaction, conversation, and experience you have had or will have is a part of your complete and total life story. If any one of the moments in your life were to be even slightly altered, you would be a completely different person. Your experience, in your body, with your unique circumstances, is a direct and total result of what you've been through and ultimately how it has affected you and shaped you.

Like my birth story, we all experience this magnitude of sadness, pain, hopelessness, loss and hurt in our lives at some level. Your personal story may be different, but those emotions and the effect these experiences have on us, happen to us all. Each and every emotion, every single thought that you have, and every decision you make, has a specific energy that comes along with it. My son was two years old when I married Cesar in August of 2013. Maddox, my brilliant warrior of a son, walked his daddy down the aisle to marry his mommy. He was wrapped in the strength and love of my husband's arms, and soon after, so was I.

I nurtured and mothered my son, hugged and adored him, and have my most precious early memories of the two of us together that are so special. I will carry them with me always. During this time of mothering and helping my son to grow into his warrior strength I started to feel a calling, like a magnet, a sort of internal voice, a need that I could not define. I wanted to help people. I wanted a broader reach to help heal more people from emotional and physical pain. I wanted to be a holistic physician. I remembered before I got pregnant with my son that an acupuncturist had healed me of endocrine system issues I had suffered for years. She cleared blockages so much so that I was able to get so easily pregnant. When my son was about two years old I made the toughest decision ever. I decided to go back to school to become a Chinese medicine and acupuncture physician. This would mean achieving a second bachelor's degree, and a master's degree, as well as an additional year at the end of it all studying for and passing four different national and state boards.

I cried all the way to school for three weeks straight. My son didn't though. Maddox was beaming with joy to play with the other kids as much as he was beaming to see Mommy at the end of the day. I did give up some time with him temporarily, but I gained a career that allowed me to have more freedom to be with my kids than any nine-to-five job ever would have allowed. Now I could provide the world and more for my children, and I oversaw my medical practice, my time, and my life.

Just before I graduated in 2015, my husband and I welcomed our sweet baby girl into the world. It was another decision-filled journey as I was so entrenched with school and the hours of studies it involved. We named her Sarai Angeline, the most angelic and beautiful name. She was a home birth for us, which was such an incredible experience. The same year she was born I opened my own holistic medicine practice as a married, business-owning, mother of two. I certainly didn't feel alone and life was good.

> *"Mommy, Mommy, I was just about to say, if you don't believe in magic, all the magic goes away"*
>
> Sarai Angeline Pena, 5 y

Sarai Angeline. This beautiful angel came into my life in May 2015. I was pregnant with her during my last year of medical school. Prior to this pregnancy, in the same year, I experienced two miscarriages. I was engulfed in school full-time, working a heavy dose of clinic hours, studying for state boards, being a mom to my son Maddox, playing the role of a fiancée and planning an entire wedding, and driving over an hour and a half to school each way daily. I was over-stressed and I knew it. Even my body knew it. I started to have severe scalp psoriasis, and joint pain. This, coupled with insomnia, and an insane drive to achieve my medical license, was a perfect example of expending more energy than I had stored up to use.

I couldn't hold the previous pregnancies. I know I was stressed and that is why. When I got pregnant with Sarai I had a choice to make. Take time off from school to nurture the pregnancy or push through and finish. I could literally see the graduation finish line. I was in my very last trimester of medical school, and I was so close to finishing. You may feel that the choice should have been clear cut and easy for me, but it was not. I spent countless hours, in the weeks following the news I was pregnant, arguing with my heart and mind, trying to make the decision I needed to make. Finally, I made a choice.

Sometimes the hardest part about making a final decision about something is the process of getting to that conclusion. The journey through decision making can be brutal, but it's amazing how you feel once you make the choice. Once it is made, a huge weight is taken off of you. You are freed of a burden, and it feels so good.

What I really wanted, when the choices were put in front of me, was to be a mother to another child. My motherly spirit took over and I decided to take the time I needed off from school to have a healthy pregnancy. I chose myself; I chose my baby, I chose life. I spent time just being pregnant. I did meditations, took walks, and fully focused on the health of my body, my mind and my womb. I nurtured my inner peace, by setting aside certain things, to achieve another and the sacrifice was worth it. I welcomed a healthy baby girl in the comfort of my own home, surrounded by midwives who honored my needs, and my husband. I labored, medication free, for fourteen hours, and pushed out another human being. She was huge! She was nine pounds, healthy, vivacious and hungry!

> *"Deciding to prioritize one thing over another was a huge part of forgiveness for me. I saw that I needed to forgive myself."*

I had lived with a constant drive to succeed, to survive, and to fight. I felt for years that life was a fight, full of lessons and hardships. The time I had spent in that messy web of discontentment had caused me to create some pretty sharp edges in my personality. I loved the world and others so much, but no-one could see through those edges. I wore them like armor, until I met the love of my life, Cesar. He refused to let go of loving me and he held on patiently until I loved him back. In many ways he saved me from myself.

When Sarai was born, and just a few months old, I went back to school, to finish what I had started out to achieve. I breastfed her during class, during clinic hours, and hired a babysitter to watch her while I studied for my boards. It wasn't easy but Sarai and I made it. I graduated, now a mother of two, a married woman, and with my medical degree!

We all know that people come into, or out of, our lives for a reason. If you are a parent, you understand the connection a parent has with their child. If you have multiple kids, you know that the connection you share with them is unique. Sarai is one of the kindest people I have ever met. Even as a toddler she taught me how to ask for forgiveness if I was too harsh with her, because she was always so quick to apologize if she misbehaved. To this day she still teaches us how to be kinder people. She is quick to say, "I'm sorry," when she gets in trouble and she lights up quickly when we say, "I forgive you." It's amazing really. I've never experienced anyone like this. My husband, my son and I all watch her kindness in awe, and I still find her to be one of the most loving people in the universe. It is an honor to be her mother and to be so very lucky to have been blessed with a son and a daughter.

It's hard to imagine how our most terrifying experiences were there to serve us, especially when you have yet to let go of resentment from your past. It's hard to imagine how the home invasion I endured, and the subsequent years of fear, crying and relationship issues, was there to serve me. It's true though. There's good and bad in this world. There are positive and negative forces, feelings and experiences. Where there is light you will always have the dark.

To know happiness, you must know it through comparing it to sadness. To embody peace, you must know fear. You may not like this, but these are the facts. At first glance this truth is frustrating and uncomfortable. But these truths are also your key to letting go. I can teach you how to use these truths to charge your life with all the inner peace, all the love and all the forgiveness you can imagine. So much of it, that it will overflow you and your entire experience of the world and your relation to it. What is this key? It is The New Forgiveness Method.

What is The New Forgiveness Method?

It is first understanding that forgiveness is a "feeling."

It's all about transforming the energy you already have.

It is transforming into joy, by transforming energy gifted to you from painful experiences.

It is a lesson on how to identify and utilize the energy gifted to you by your emotions.

It is using your emotions as fuel to achieve your life's greatest desires.

It is cultivation of personal healing by recognizing that forgiveness is within you and is for you.

It is learning the skills you need to use your energy as fuel to achieve your dreams.

It is gratitude for those who hurt you, by seeing the bigger picture.

It is understanding that there is a purpose for every experience in your life.

It is believing that your purpose is to achieve your greatest happiness.

The New Forgiveness

SIX

Energy: The Key to Unlocking Forgiveness

What's really causing the pain in your body? That poking, pinching, throbbing pain that presses on the inside of your skull so hard it feels like your head may just pop right open. Being trained as an eastern medicine physician I was taught medically to look at the entire body as one system, taking a very holistic approach to solving the mystery of the body's imbalances. One major part of the diagnosis process in holistic medicine is labeled, "Listening." In order to be a good holistic physician, one must learn to be a good listener.

Although life looked like it was going my way, I started to feel exhausted both mentally and physically. Like most westerners, when it came to any amount of pain, I also wanted a quick fix. I tried over the counter medications, more rest, less coffee - nothing worked at all. I was running my own acupuncture and herbal medicine practice, and for a long time I had been feeling a lack of something. I had a happy heart. I felt gratitude for my life. I had love for my husband, and we were getting along very well at the time. My home felt like a home and my children were thriving. They were happy and were very loving to me and my husband. My practice was doing well, as in making good money, clients were healing, and I had flexibility in my schedule. So what could be making me feel so down? Why was I full of relentless and sorrowful thoughts? What was causing my severe insomnia?

My children were happy going to summer camp. They would rush out the door saying, "Hurry Mommy, we are going to be late!" For some reason though, I was still very anxious and felt that I needed to get to my practice to open the doors and get to my voicemails, take care of marketing, get to that networking event and even to working on this book. Then I realized exactly what was off for me. I was dealing with two simultaneous factors. One factor was those old shoved down memories that still caused my heart to ache with hatred for the past and the person who hurt me, and another factor was my own imbalance as a mom in my day-to-day dealings. I was just too darn busy. Both of these factors needed attention, and both needed to change.

I missed my kids. I wasn't spending the time with them that I needed. They may have been happy with the time we had together, but I wasn't filling my motherly cup; I mattered too. I closed my practice the next day. Yes, I cancelled all my patients, took my daughter out of school, and we had a much overdue mommy and me day. We did whatever we wanted moment by moment. We watched The Nutcracker on Netflix, went to lunch together, got our nails done, shopped for a new wallet for her and played with Barbies.

Since that day I have had many Mommy and me days with both of my kids. Each school year they both get to pick two days where we stay home together and enjoy the moment. The energy behind this one decision I made propelled me to understanding that taking the time I needed with my kids was worth way more than any amount of money I was losing by closing down my practice for a day. I had more energy to give when I did go back to my practice. I forgave myself for not doing it sooner and committed to continuing the tradition. Why not? It felt so good!

On our next Mommy and me day, my daughter, now just four years old at the time, actually begged to go to my office with me. She really wanted to see what Mommy did. She said, "Mommy, I want to watch you treat a patient." That afternoon she sat quietly, and she watched her Mommy treat a patient with cupping therapy, acupuncture and homeopathic injections. From this little girl, with inquisitive eyes and curiosity, the questions emerged. She asked about holistic medicine.

About an hour later as we sat in my office, I was finishing up for the day and she poked her head up from her princess coloring book and said, "Mommy, you're the best doctor, and I love you." Then she put her head and thoughts back to her coloring and the moment passed. That night I got more hugs and more attention from her than I had in the weeks preceding. Then it occurred to me, while I did still have a slight underlying headache that persisted, the majority of my head pain was completely gone. Not only that, but I also felt better about my life, my business, my family and my choices. All I did differently was look at what was out of balance and fixed it, with one day of spending life's biggest commodity with my child, time.

Stress is a big conversation in all fields of medicine because of the science and research that has been done regarding how stress affects the body and the mind. We can all agree that the more stressed you are the less energy you have, right? Then can you also see how energy can help you heal? There are countless bits of information now on how to feel good, many self-help books, audio recordings, speakers, seminars, self-help meditations, etc. It goes to wonder then, with so much education out there on exactly how to feel at peace, why there is still so little peace at all.

Having a happy heart and inner joy does not mean you will not have contemplative, lonely or depressed days. It's not our purpose in the human experience to be in pure bliss existentially without ever feeling lonely or confused. It's definitely part of the gamut of emotions we have to deal with in our human experience. Embracing these life experiences has helped me to understand this. Have you noticed that nothing ever stays the same? Even things that seem to go on endlessly, without change, do eventually change.

When you feel happy, and when you feel calm in your life, it feels good until something comes along to upset that balance, right? That changes your experience of joy and you now feel depressed, angry, hopeless or unforgiving. The good news is the law of never-ending change applies in both areas. When things change in your life, or inside of you emotionally, there is a feeling of imbalance, but this imbalance is also temporary. All things flow and change so knowing that change is imminent is part of embracing life and all its many faceted sides. This should bring you some solace. Look up, the bright side is just around the corner, if not already staring you in the face.

I was able to see the imbalance of energy with my kids, and I was able to fix it with spending more time with them. But there was something else prodding at me. There was something lingering deeper in my consciousness and even deeper in my cells. It was the hatred and resentment I still harbored from the past. I am sorry to tell you this but you can never shove it down far enough to forget these emotions. You have to deal with your past or you will suffer from it every day at your own hand.

I became obsessed with achieving forgiveness by applying the eastern medicine philosophy of how energy is created and supplied by our emotions from our experiences. I wanted to dive deep into understanding the science of how emotions create energy in order to understand how to achieve forgiveness. Little did I know that I was about to figure it all out. A new hardship was coming my way and it changed everything. I woke up because of it, and the secret to transforming hatred into joy and to transforming resentment into forgiveness was revealed.

If something is your destiny you will feel it deep inside of you. If something is your destiny it is meant for you. A few years into my now busy practice, I truly enjoyed treating patients but there it was again. That lingering, shoulder-tapping voice inside of me, that told me there was more I needed to do. There was that entrepreneurial spirit taking over again. I kept feeling a deep sense of knowing that building a busy medical practice and treating patients, one by one, one hour at a time, was not a stopping point in my journey to help more people. I suddenly realized one day, that once again, I was about to recreate myself. Only this time it was different. For the first time in my life journey, and in my search for my sense of self, as it comes to a career, I knew I needed to continue to grow for the benefit and healing of others. I knew that I could not reach the sheer amount of people I wanted to if I stayed in my treatment room for the next twenty years treating one patient at a time.

I knew I was about to make another bold move to endeavor to move forward and onward once again. I sat with my husband, ever so supportive, yet ever so concerned with my ambition and constant underlying discontent to stay in the comfort of stability for too long. By the end of the conversation, he understood that I needed to pursue bigger and greater things. I needed to help the world. I needed more time with my kids and I needed more time with him. I knew my inner "happy" would cry incessantly for release if I didn't listen to my gut and to my heart.

I knew this, but I also did something else, I honored this. Because of my willingness to listen to my heart and make sometimes uncomfortable but necessary changes, here we were. Little did I know that the catalyst for change for this ground-breaking moment in my life was just around the corner. It wasn't about to happen for my benefit alone. It was about to happen for the benefit of all, for the benefit of every reader of this book, for the benefit of mankind. It propelled me into my calling and propelled me into every moment that led to my writing this book. The "It" I refer to, is the conniving desire of someone trying to hurt me and my business, someone backhanded and dishonest. I didn't know it then, but I soon found out that this specific occurrence would be the fuel for change in my life, and the exact fuel I needed to achieve the greatest gift of all, forgiveness.

This was my wake up. It was my new beginning emotionally, spiritually, and in every way possible. It was the beginning of learning how to transform the energy that comes from the force and magnitude of our emotions created from our experiences. This is the part where you are going to learn how to transform your deepest hurt into only that which serves you well, love.

By the time I was forty I was three years into my holistic medicine practice. I was running the business on my own and renting space out of a western medical doctor's practice, which was always my dream, to bring both sides of medicine together.

"There's an undeniable connection between all of us. It's like a silver cord going from one human being to another, that continues until we are all just one interconnected web of love."

It was years after my home invasion that once again my skills of maintaining happiness were put to the test. Still whirling with post-traumatic stress disorder from the incident years ago, I was faced yet again with betrayal, but this time it was at the hands of a local business owner in town, who I will call Heather. One day,

I had an idea, a glorious and wondrous idea. I discussed my idea with some friends that were also in similar holistic healing practices. I envisioned what I called a Holistic Hospital. It would be a building where practitioners of all modalities would have a practice under one roof. It would be a place where a patient could have all of their medical needs met from a holistic modality standpoint. Of course an endeavor like this would take backing, funding, partners, and a great team of licensed healers.

After a few months of discussing this idea with other like-minded practitioners a few of us met at a restaurant to discuss business. Heather was part of this meeting. We wanted to talk about how we may be able to support each other business-wise. I fully respected and trusted her as well as the other practitioners at the table. At this meeting we discussed this holistic hospital idea. As we sipped on sake and enjoyed our sushi, we began our meeting. I explained to them that I would love to have a building that would be solely dedicated to holistic practitioners, with one main front reception area, serving and guiding patients to each practitioner's office. We would work together to treat patients in one space and run our own practices respectively. I explained that we would need some investors and that I already had holistic practitioners on board with the project who eagerly wished to rent space in this new holistic hospital.

Heather lit up, jumped right in, and advised us that she was already approved for over one million dollars to build a new space. This idea was exactly what she wanted to do too. I knew that she had been thinking along these same lines for a long time. She had been trying to have a practice where she would have many different practitioners in her space. I knew for many years that practitioners of many modalities would come and go in her business. I knew that she was a businessperson and that she had the financial means for a project of this magnitude.

We sent text messages back and forth within the group as we found different possible retail spaces that may work for our project. We also discussed purchasing land and then building out a space. A couple of weeks went by, and I heard nothing from her. Then I decided to go to a networking event where she showed up. She ignored me as if we didn't know each other. There was a microphone on a stage in front of the room where each businessperson had a chance to get up and promote themselves and their business. No sooner did she walk in the front door she jumped the line and got right up on that stage for a big announcement.

Without skipping a beat, looking slightly past me to not meet my eye, she made a statement to the entire group. She said that she was looking to open a new space that would be like a holistic hospital. She then went on to describe in detail, word for word, exactly what I had told her. She painted a direct picture of the vision I had shared and the one we had been working on together and made it look like it was her idea alone. I was out.

She didn't say my name, acknowledge my involvement, or in any way honor my part in the idea. I had been backhanded. I had been slighted. I had been overlooked, overstepped, and overused for my ideas. I had trusted this person and I was thrown out like garbage. We never spoke again, and all referrals stopped. I had had people in town saying for years that she was not to be trusted. They warned me of her unscrupulous ways but it wasn't my experience of her so I had to learn on my own. I had ignored all the warnings because I wanted to trust her. So, what did I do?

I got angry! I could feel the heat rising. I could feel my head getting hot and my face getting red. I could feel my fingers sweating, my lips pursing together and my teeth grinding. I was throwing daggers at her with my eyes. I had to get out of there. That same day I saw social media posts from her office announcing this "new" idea. I was even told by a mutual business contact of ours that she had asked if I was mad at her. Heather said that she knew I would be mad, even though we had, at that time, and to this day, never spoken since the lunch meeting where we discussed going into business together. She knew exactly what she had done.

I spent two weeks being extremely angry. I mean every day, every minute, and every second of my life, for two weeks straight I was mad. I was deep down cellular-level mad. I was so angry that I couldn't stop talking about it. I couldn't stop thinking about it. Two weeks is a long time to have such an intense emotion of hatred and resentment. That, piled on top of the pain I had still yet to heal from the home invasion years ago, was enough to wake me up. While I was feeling this immense amount of hatred toward Heather I decided to begin with a single thought. How can I feel better and get past this?

I had read self-help books in the past, specifically on the topic of forgiveness, about letting go, about moving forward from an experience in some optimistic and self-serving way. Nothing really worked, not from the aspect of how these books and speakers wrote steps to forgiveness. It didn't work; I didn't feel better, not in my heart, not in my mind and I was still angry. There I sat, on my couch with anger. Lots and lots of anger. Then, BOOM! A beam of understanding struck through me like a lightning bolt.

Suddenly something strange and magnificent happened! I was sitting on my couch, full of anger, and worst of all defeat, as well as embarrassment from all the gossiping I had been doing. I had felt powerless. But suddenly now I felt something else, something new. I felt something I had never felt in my entire life, something I had never before tapped into. *I felt this emotion of anger, as just ENERGY!* Could I forgive her and now suddenly feel this immense joy? Yes, I did.

The years I spent face-planting into Chinese medicine books, learning about qi, energy, and emotional forces, flooded my brain, filled my heart and inspired my spirit all at once. I was enlightened. I felt the literal ball of energy in my body like a force I could now completely control, and I began to immediately move it from my gut as if I could take this ball of energy and move it rapidly through my fingertips at will.

It felt like I could throw this ball in any direction, and with force! This energy was created from the hurt and the hatred I felt by the betrayal of her stealing my idea, but it was transformed into love in a split second of awareness. That's a lot of energy! Then it dawned on me - could I somehow use it for good? Could this be the feeling of forgiveness? Heck yes, it could. I had energy and because it was energy from anger, I had a lot of it. I needed to use it and I needed to use it now. This was the catalyst for more change in my life. This caused my forgiveness awakening.

What seemed like a sudden epiphany was really a cultivation of all my years of training in Chinese medicine. It was a culmination of hundreds, if not over a thousand hours of reading and applying the law of emotional energy in the process of healing. I had spent most of my adult life learning about energy, the human body, and the science behind change.

All the previous years, and up to that moment, I had felt that I didn't have the time or the energy to do any charity work. I had no energy to make a real impact on the lives of others. I wanted to, but I was legitimately fatigued from working so hard as a wife, mother and business owner so no one could blame me for running out of time or steam at the end of any given day. But now with the massive amount of energy that came with my anger, I realized I could use it.

Sitting on my couch in defeat and anger, I suddenly felt a rush of inspiration. I had talked in the past with a fellow doctor, friend and production company owner about doing some work to help others. I had done a few talk shows in the past with her as well as some speaker training. I had always wanted to work with her in some way, but I just couldn't see past my ambitions to grow my medical practice and help people heal, one hour, one patient at a time, but now I could see clear as a spring river. Clarity came to me directly through my pain, I just had to twist it and use the energy it provided me for the greater good. My hurt and anger that was caused by being passed over in a business transaction was suddenly the most exciting inspiration for change, not only in my life, but soon also in the life of others.

Full of boundless energy, and solely because of this energy, I made the call that changed my path forever. I called Dr. Shelley Plumb, at Plumb Talk Productions, and I told her that I was ready to start changing the world with her. At that moment, "The Kindness Project Worldwide" was off the ground. It was a brainchild of ours together, but we had not created it yet. Suddenly, and with a force of positivity and excitement, I was ready! And to my relief, so was she! It was like she was about to pick up the phone and call me at the same time. This was absolutely a divine intervention and certainly   impecca- ble timing.

The energy gained with this ability to forgive more quickly, and to see the reason behind the people and circumstances that hurt us, can power and light up the world. I began co-hosting a television show called "The Kindness Project Worldwide" with Dr. Shelley Plumb. I became the co-host of a show that had one sole purpose, to highlight love and spread kindness to others. I became an active member of my local Rotary Club. I traveled on a whim of desire with Shelley to the Bahamas after Hurricane Dorian. It was the beginning of something magnificent and it all started because someone betrayed me, and I used the energy from that hurt for good.

Without that betrayal I wouldn't be hosting the show, I wouldn't be writing this book, I wouldn't be alive in the most forgiving way possible. I am thankful for this experience and therefore fully forgive Heather. Not only that, but I genuinely feel gratitude for the situation. Forgiveness can be, and is, seeing and understanding that the hurt someone caused you was exactly what you needed to create and achieve wondrous, happy and new experiences in your life.

In Chinese medicine, using energy to fuel disease or create wellness is referred to as transforming qi. *Energy is the key to unlocking forgiveness.* There are times you need to forgive yourself and times you need to forgive someone else. Either way, using the energy behind your decisions is an accessible tool you can use to achieve this forgiveness. Kindness is the most accessible and easiest form of beginning to unlock forgiveness. Kindness can spark change in your life, in your body, and affect how you experience everything.

**Kindness is a key to embracing
your extraordinary inner joy.**

FIRST: Be kind to yourself.
SECOND: Extend kindness to others.
REWARD: Unlocking the door to forgiveness
using kindness as the key.

THE BREAK DOWN
Transformation of Energy to Achieve Forgiveness

1. You are betrayed, and you get very angry because of the fear, trauma or betrayal you just experienced.

2. You start gossiping about the terrible experience you had, looking for others to understand by being as hurt or as angry as you are.

3. You may settle into this hatred just long enough to start letting the resentment fester. Once this happens, the inner sadness and depression can take over your emotional wellbeing.

Whatever your specific trauma may be, the way we feel emotions in our body is propelled by the specific energetic force they create. In the case of my being betrayed in business, I experienced anger and rage. But from that I was awakened to that energy ball inside of me. Suddenly all my training about qi and how emotions are just levels of energy, woke me up and I recognized my emotions as a gift, a great big ball of qi, delivered to me from the hatred that was swirling and growing in my belly.

I had a lot of anger, so I also had a great big ball of qi, I had fuel. I had energy! What I really had was a gift. I had fuel, energy, and focus for the eventual healing of myself and others. I actually got excited because I was so full of energy, and full of focus, I was finally driven to make a call to do something wondrous. This call was fueled solely by the energy created by the betrayal of another. With my good friend, we started "The Kindness Project World-wide," right then and there, over a phone call.

I became thankful for the betrayal, and can say, "Thank you," to that person. I forgive them. Are you listening? This is The New Forgiveness. *You have complete control over how you move through your experiences and how you move past them. Even more exciting, you now know that you do have control over your energy, you just have to wake up to it.*

This is a common progress of emotions when we are hurt. Look how I used this pain, anger and hatred to transform from hatred into forgiveness. I used the energy that was created from anger to get off the couch and find a better way to use that energy and to personally feel better within myself.

SEVEN

The Effect Emotions Have on Your Qi Using Your Emotions as Fuel

As a licensed acupuncturist, herbalist and holistic practitioner I have immense training in the true foundations of Chinese medicine. I want to share with you some very important teachings about emotions and the lifelong effect they can have on your physical health. The root of Chinese medicine begins thousands of years ago and has to do with one single concept, the energy created by our emotions and experiences. That concept of energy is loosely translated as qi. For this book when I talk about qi, it represents energy and life force. Qi represents the energy created when you experience specific emotions. Before I can teach you how to use your energy to create forgiveness, you must first understand what qi "energy" is, and how it affects you.

The Chinese understood that qi was vital to life, meaning

that a life void of qi equals death. They knew that qi was a life force that ran through the veins of human life and that perfect health meant balanced qi. Qi is more than just a physical disease or healthy life experience. The Chinese realized that the human body and the mind were fully intertwined. Like blood flowing through your blood vessels, qi was flowing though vessels they called meridians. They found a way to impact qi, and a way to revitalize our experience of imbalance and disease in the body, using acupuncture. This is impressive for a therapeutic technique that is thousands of years old, and still exists in its original form today.

Why is acupuncture so successful at treating imbalances, especially regarding your emotions, and your state of physical health? Well, your emotions have a very specific impact on your body, so specific in fact, that microscopic points can be stimulated on the human body to encourage a release of a targeted emotion. Application of the proper acupuncture technique can even detoxify an organ system. The Chinese discovered the specific energetic effect behind every emotion, and they figured out exactly what organ in the human body was affected by that emotion. This is genius if you ask me. Furthermore, they discovered that the symptoms a patient was exhibiting matched specific current or past emotional traumas that occurred over the course of that patient's lifetime. Chinese medicine is a therapy that is holistic. Holistic medicine takes a whole-body approach to diagnosis and treatment planning, most definitely never undermining the significance of a patient's emotions and state of mind. If you understand how energy can affect your body and your health, then you can see how it can be transformed by you, in any way that you want. If you are willing to learn, to try, and to focus, you can do it.

It took over forty years of life on this earth, nine years of schooling, years of clinical experience, and a busy licensed practice for me to understand firsthand how our thoughts can turn to energy and how that energy shapes our health. Once you understand how that energy affects your health, you can then learn to take it one step further. You can learn how to harness that energy and use it, and I am going to teach you how.

Having well trained, excellent listening skills are such a vital part of the diagnostic process in any holistic medicine practice. So much so that, without listening, and being formally trained to read between the lines and listen for specific word cues, the physician would not be able to choose the correct acupuncture point or herbal formula. In my practice I don't always get to know what the long-term effects of the treatments are on my patients, but once in a while they put it in writing and it almost always has to do with their gratitude for feeling heard, and for my listening to them. Here are a few letters I received.

"Dear Sweet Dr. Caroline,
You have changed my life in ways I didn't realize could be possible. You are my angel on earth. No matter where life takes us, you will live in my heart forever! Words cannot express how grateful I am for you!!"

"Dear Caroline,
Thank you for being there for me. You are such a great listener, and you are the true asset of healing, physically and emotionally. I thank God that my daughter found you for me. I feel so connected to you. Also Caroline, your friendship means so much to me!"

"Dear Caroline,
I wanted you to know how much I have appreciated you. Not only are you so very skilled at your work, but you're caring, and your giving nature comes through. I hope if you relocate that you will forward that info. Don't give up and follow your heart!

It wasn't until I had my clinical practice and really started treating patients on a regular basis that I started to see the effects of how healing emotions could change a person's experience in their own body. Everyone wants to feel loved, and everyone wants to feel hope, everyone. This is some insight to help you understand how much your emotions affect your body, mind, spirit and physical health.

There are five main organ systems at the root of Chinese medicine. Each of these five organs are paired with their matching counterpart. The five main yin organs are the liver, heart, spleen, lung, and kidney. Each Yin organ has its opposite organ match, which are all Yang organs. See the chart below:

Organ Pairs:	Emotions
Liver *pairs with* Gallbladder	Anger, Frustration, Jealousy, Envy Poor Decision Making
Heart *pairs with* Small Intestine	Joy, Hate and Anxious Feelings Meanness and Impatience
Spleen *pairs with* Stomach	Worry, Anxiety, Overthinking, Mistrust
Lung *pairs with* Large Intestine	Sadness, Grief and Depression
Kidney *pairs with* Urinary Bladder	Fear of attack, or feeling frightened constantly

The Liver/Gallbladder Pair

Anger affects the liver. The emotion of anger is an emotion just like any other. In the world of healing, emotions are created equal, in the sense that they are just energy. Although emotions certainly don't feel equal, such as comparing joy with anger, one may feel more or less significant, but it is energy all the same.

For example, joy and anger have the same significance in the body. And yes, that would imply that on an emotional level, you can even have too much or too little joy. But we'll get to that later when we start to talk about the heart. When you get angry what happens inside of your body, especially if you hold onto anger for too long? Think about it. Anger turns to irritability. Your liver channel, otherwise known as your liver meridian, is affected and you may experience headaches, tendon or muscle pain, and especially problems with making decisions. If you are experiencing these symptoms, then the energy that's affecting you the most will coincide with these organs, the liver and gallbladder. Another great example is when you are doing really great. You're working hard, you're encouraged and feeling accomplished. The term comes to mind, "You're on fire!" This is great, as long as you have enough fire, or qi, to burn.

Fire is yang energy. It is as wonderful as it is powerful and burns upwards, allowing you to achieve amazing feats. But if you let your fire burn for too long, without necessary rest, and without taking a break to rejuvenate, then your fire will either burn out or rage out of control. Either way, you'll be, as we say, "Burnt out," and who wants that.

The Kidney/Urinary Bladder Pair

The kidneys and urinary bladder have very specific emotions attached to them, fear and fright. If you have a panic disorder then you're definitely out of balance in these specific organs, or the flow of these meridians associated with those organs can be off in a very big way. Panic attacks don't happen for "no reason at all." Meridians are channels where qi and yin flow. Think of meridians like blood vessels. If they are blocked you will feel pain, discomfort and lack of wellness within your body system.

You can see this in the science of western medicine easily. The experience of sudden fear or fright may cause you to urinate, your eyes to dilate, your heart to palpate and then soon after you may lose your ability to hold a peaceful state of mind. If you have issues with your organs it can work the opposite way too. What I mean by this is if you have kidney or urinary bladder issues, you may suffer from panic disorders, frequent urination, and even sexual dysfunction and certainly have some level of low back pain if the kidneys are involved.

If you have any of the above symptoms, you need to investigate your past and see what frightened you. See if you can deal with it and try to let it go. In my acupuncture practice I insert needles into specific points to help rebalance the qi of these meridians. Sometimes patients have a huge emotional release on the treatment table. Sometimes the tears just start to flow, and then their symptoms fall away and they finally have the best night's sleep, sometimes in years. If you feel that the hurt and the trauma you have experienced is just too hard to let go of, then use what I teach you in this book to transform the energy behind that experience into something that will serve you well.

I know it can be done because I did it myself. To transform energy, you first must define it, find it, see it, and feel it inside of you. Once you identify the feeling or emotion, then you use that feeling or emotion as energy and as fuel. The guided meditation at the end of this book helps you to experience this transformative energy. Practice makes perfect my friend. Practice and cultivate the ability to apply this method to any and all experiences in your life.

The Lungs/Large Intestine Pair

The lungs and the large intestines are attached to sadness and grief. If you grieve for too long you can have very low energy, shortness of breath, constipation or feelings of heaviness in the chest. The lungs also govern the skin so long periods of sadness or grief can cause you to have skin issues, anywhere from itching internally or under the skin, to rashes.

Many times, rashes are relentless and don't go away under medical treatment because there's no pill to resolve your sadness or grief. The New Forgiveness Method is a technique to help you use the energy you have from your painful experiences to transform yourself and your life. Forgiveness then follows, as does the possible healing of your skin rashes.

The Stomach/Spleen Pair

The stomach and spleen have unique emotions attached to them. As an acupuncture physician, in my practice, this is the one I see humanity suffering from the most, excessive worry and overthinking. Some people call that being pensive. There is a healthy amount of staring off into space and thinking that can be good for you but if you overthink or over worry for too long, it really affects your body. When a patient comes into my practice and tells me they have poor digestion, feels bloated, have loose stools, can't think straight and are constantly fatigued then I know automatically to treat the stomach and spleen meridians.

Do you have a change of appetite, or hunger with no desire to eat? Are you overeating? If you have any of these symptoms, then you may be experiencing an imbalance in these meridians. Thinking too much can cause all of the above symptoms. Sometimes a few good acupuncture sessions and a nice relaxing meditation can resolve these issues.

The Heart/Small Intestine Pair

Joy, hate, meanness, and impatience all affect these meridians. Wow, joy? How can that be a "bad" emotion? The foundations of Chinese medicine found that there was always a necessary balance in life, a nature of all things. This was something they called the relationship between yin and yang. Think about someone who suddenly finds out they won the lottery. They are so overjoyed that their heart qi is suddenly out of balance, and they die of a heart attack still holding the winning ticket. It's a harsh example but it's true.

Balance is always the body's greatest desire. The body's desire is to always achieve a state of homeostasis, otherwise known as balance. Taken out of balance, whether it is short term or long term (like holding onto an emotion for years) means that you won't feel complete until you are balanced once again, until you are healed and feel whole.

Hate, meanness, and impatience are so fiercely related to the heart almost everyone reading this book can relate, the worst of which is the emotion of hatred. When you hate someone, so intensely hate someone, it leads directly to anxiety. If you tend to suffer from severe depression, anxiety, insomnia, have heart palpitations or just feel like you have mental restlessness then look at your intestinal health, the health of your heart and the resentment you may be harboring. Hatred only poisons you. I am sorry to tell you this, but your hatred adds not one single ounce of suffering to the one who hurt you.

What is at the core of my message? Forgiveness is. Forgiveness of yourself, of others, of the past, and of your current state of mind is the open door to a peaceful life. Peace lives in your heart. Whether you feel peaceful or not, peace is stored there, you just have to open the door. When the idea of forgiveness is too much for you to bear, then use the powerhouse of stored energy from your emotions to move forward. Why not? You do want to feel better, right? You must want it. No one can make you feel better, and no one can make you want to feel better. You are, in the end, the one who decides to sink or swim, rise or fall, succeed or fail or continue or stop this journey.

From a health standpoint, when you have a specific emotion your organs are going to be affected. Then you will begin to experience physical symptoms in your body that can get worse and worse with time, especially if the emotion is not balanced and resolved. Some examples of the physical symptoms caused by unresolved emotions are fatigue, unexplained all over body pain, insomnia, social shyness, liver and kidney disease, digestive issues, memory loss, and neuropathic issues to name a few. Do I have your attention now?

> Remember one thing, life is for living! You are here to live. So, use this book as a significant piece to your complicated healing puzzle. Learn all you can about energy and the power of forgiveness. Your heart just might get so full you will finally experience the joy you've craved for so long. You may break open. You just might break free and be healed.

Be gentle with yourself, the act of being kind is medicine all in itself. The New Forgiveness is a powerful concept. Integrated and intertwined with the inner desires of all mankind, is peace. The New Forgiveness is a tangible and achievable concept. You absolutely can get in the way of your own healing. Don't be a naysayer, be a wide-open willing player in this game of forgiveness. Give it all you've got; I promise you can get better.

Many people feel that forgiveness doesn't work for them and that's how I felt for most of my life. I was holding very tightly onto "no, I am not forgiving some people who hurt the core of my being." I held onto that "no" for years. I was festering "no" like it was a part of me that was keeping me safe but it wasn't.

"Hatred is just like poison, and forgiveness is the cure."

EIGHT

The Energy Waterfall

Like a waterfall crashing over a cliff, picking up energy as it whispers its way towards the earth's gravitational pull, your emotions mimic this whimsical relationship of science and spirit, picking up energy as it crashes downward. I call this the "Energy Waterfall". What this represents is how your emotions start and then build on one another, feeding on each other. Fear and anger quickly "rage" out of control quite like when we say a waterfall is "raging out of control." Fear is an emotion that is felt the deepest inside of us, with the most momentum and force. Fear is instant and settles deep in our psyche quickly showing physical effects in disease and fatigue. Left unattended, the emotion of fear grows in the body like a cancer and affects your life, your thoughts and your physical wellbeing.

Harboring resentment is equally as damaging, but it takes on a much slower approach to unrest. It festers and collides constantly with your deepest desires for peace. It slowly unravels good relationships, as you are constantly convinced that forgiveness is impossible, which leads you to unrest, allowing the resentment to continue to grow.

If you have ever been hurt deeply, suffered from emotional trauma, and experienced hatred in your heart, then listen up. For many years I was absolutely overwhelmed with the desire to find forgiveness for those who hurt me so badly. I was obsessed with finding a way to heal my otherwise loving and sympathetic heart. I had post-traumatic stress disorder from some of those experiences. My refusal to let go had caused a constant replay of past events. Repeatedly I would relive them in my mind.

My past and what happened, it hurt me deeply. It plastered fear in my heart, and hatred took over my soul. I could literally feel the hatred pumping through my veins. I knew there was no easy fix to how I felt because it seemed to me that the betrayal was too much to bear, so my heart pounded in rage.

I tried so hard, I cried so hard, and it didn't work. Just forgive, just let it go. It was impossible. I could not pretend I felt better, I felt how I felt, but there had to be another way. The statement, "Forgiveness is for you, not them," would just make me angrier, because it wasn't working. I could see how the hatred was only poisoning me, and not them. I could feel that the hatred wasn't protecting me as I searched desperately for a cure to the resentment in my heart.

The hatred and resentment had a trickle-down effect on my life, and about broke up my marriage. The years of lying in defeat, hiding in my closet, tear soaking the carpet, showed me that there had to be another way to let this go. I had tried all the traditional healing methods I could find. Counseling, meditation, yoga, books, audio recordings, worksheets, religion, you name it, I tried it! And when I say years, I mean years of trying very hard to let it go. Its's a lot to bear.

Letting go of hatred is challenging if the person who hurt you is no longer in your life and has no reason to be. Another test of resiliency, finding your inner peace, and joy, is when you must keep the door cracked open to that person in some way. This happens when the person who hurt you is a family member, or maybe they are someone very special to someone else you love. You can't just push them away; you must deal with it because of the love you have for someone else.

In one case for me, it was a close family member of a close family member of mine. Loving this person I have in my life, meant finding ways to navigate through hatred, and find a way to open a door for the person who hurt me. I never got to run from this forgiveness journey, so it was meant to be.

"It was meant to be." Just the sound of it fills me with emotion almost immediately. Even if you believe that all the situations in your life are meant to be, it still leaves an "ouch" with its sound, like an echo bouncing off the walls of a cave coming back with a painful slap. It's an echo reminding you, repeatedly, that this hurt is there to serve you, to make you a better person and to help you be a master forgiver. The darker forces that are out there, they don't want you to wake up into forgiveness, because the only control they have over you is hatred and fear. ***Love is the answer.***

It takes courage to tell your story. It is taking courage for me now, but in the process, the most amazing energy can fill you up. When you achieve forgiveness, you feel like you can soar, like you can fly, like you can finally inhale and breathe in the deepest healing breath. You can finally rest, rejuvenate, and let it all go. I have escaped the painful echoes inside my sacred internal cave. For me, the cave was my closet, the closet that held me tightly in solace through all those tears for all those years. One day, I walked in the house right to that closet and gathered up that tear-soaked rug. I tossed it in the garbage, and it was so empowering. I am grateful for that rug, but I no longer have use for it. I've forgiven and I have finally dried my tears from my painful past.

9 Steps to Understanding the Energy Waterfall

1. You are traumatized and deeply hurt.

2. Imaging that your sequence of emotions place you at the top of a mountain looking over a waterfall, full of emotion.

3. You are so hurt and become so angry and full of hatred for someone that the hatred pours over the wa-

terfall bearing downward, gaining momentum, growing in force and energy.

4. Those emotions fester and take up your mind space, flooding your thoughts so greatly that you may even begin to gossip to others about what happened.

5. You begin looking for others to be as angry as you are! When they are not, this resentment is added to the original hurt, and adds a more powerful flow to the waterfall as it continues to crash downward.

6. You lose sleep, or have nightmares followed with a waking sense of malaise and fatigue that you cannot shake, no matter how much sleep you may get. The waterfall rages on, almost ready to crash on the rocks below.

7. The anger grows inside of you. Your other relationships are affected, and you lose hope that forgiveness is even possible.

8. You are lost and cannot get past it. You either refuse to forgive the hurt or simply cannot, either way, your discontent pours over the waterfall, now full of more power and more rage. The waves of emotion crash on the chaotic ground and earth below.

9. Crash! You hit rock bottom! **The impact of your emotions hitting rock bottom are so loud, you are left with two decisions. You can hit rock bottom, stay there and drown, or you can forgive.**

It's ok if you chose defeat in the past. The hurt was, or still feels, too painful to let go of and to forgive. If you are ready to feel better, be happier, and rid yourself of so many physical symptoms and pain, then choose healing today. Follow my step-by-step guide to The New Forgiveness, which I will go over in chapter eleven. What do you have to lose, just your resentment right? Are you ready to catch your breath?

For many moons, there have been teachings that every-thing is there to serve us, to teach us, and to help us grow. To this end I do agree, but I also believe strongly that sometimes things just suck, through no fault of our own, and we just need to get out of that place, moment, job, relationship, city, mindset, whatever it may be. I used to believe that I attracted situations to myself, but now, while this can and does hold true in many instances, I also believe that we are NOT responsible for the behaviors of those around us.

If you are looking for happiness, look no further than in your own mirror. Happiness has been inside of you all along. No one can take it from you. You can only give it away. Sometimes rock bottom can be the most beautiful place. It's at rock bottom where I have found the most beauty and peace in life. It can be a gift, so don't be ashamed of your feelings, reactions or your past. Be willing to move forward because nothing ever stays the same, that's a guarantee.

Lastly, and most importantly, true forgiveness is letting go of believing you can have a better past. When you do move forward, things in your life become more than you ever could have imagined. You will look back and realize that you never would have stepped into your own truth, if that horrible thing hadn't happened to you. Imagine saying to yourself, or the person that hurt you so much, not only thank you, but I forgive you, because without what you did to me, I would not be able to live my dream now, and right now I am the best and highest version of myself that I have ever been.

*"Forgiveness is letting go of believing
you can have a better past."*

The New Forgiveness

NINE

You Have a Purpose

You have a purpose. You really are unique by design, and by design you are the only person on earth just like you. Being you is incredible. I often think that if any single person on this earth were to tell their life story it would seem almost unbelievable. We don't tend to think or realize that each person, no matter what they have or don't have, no matter what our perception of their reality is, that they do have pain and hurt they've had to overcome. They may even still be in the process of overcoming past trauma, but whatever their circumstance may be, we are never alone in our struggles, and we are certainly not alone in our virtues, successes and our happiness either.

Be present enough in your own life that you can hear your inner voice. If you have lost hope, then what you merely lack is a clear vision. What is your vision? When is it time to do what you need to do? How long will you wait to embody your inner joy? How long will you blame others for your failure to forgive? You do not have to wait any longer. You can take off running or start slow, the key is that you do decide to start.

So, what now? How do you deal with your feelings once you have forgiven the offense or the offender? Transforming energy, and the ability to do so, feels almost magical in nature. This can also make it challenging to achieve happiness when you're dealing with deeper or more rooted past offenses that you've endured. For almost nine years I harbored so much resentment from my home invasion experience that at times I would fantasize about how it would feel to forgive. I thought it would be some fantastical experience, this feeling of letting go, something like a magical box opening while angelic doves flew toward the sky.

Ok, well maybe I never really envisioned this when I was in the process of forgiving, but once I forgave, I realized that this vision was pretty close to the feeling I was expecting to have. I did feel peace and calm in my heart along with a glorious openness within myself, now ready to be filled with love in place of the hatred that has now been healed.

Forgiveness does not always go hand in hand with how you feel about actually being around that person. You now have control over your forgiveness. You have forgiven and that is huge! You cannot necessarily control how you feel about reconciling.

Forgiveness does not require you to spend time with the person you have forgiven. Forgiveness does not require reconciliation.

Even if they are a person in your close inner circle, your tribe if you will, you do not have to spend time with them just because someone you love expects it of you. Most of the time, doing something out of a sense of obligation is not loving yourself and it is certainly not loving them. It's just the truth. When you've achieved forgiveness your internal experience changes, how you personally feel is completely different. Forgiveness is about you, and how you feel living in your body. It's about your experience emotionally and spiritually. When this happens, you'll know it. You will know it because you will feel it.

For me, I can take deep breaths for the first time in many years. I can exhale and feel love. I can pray for those who hurt me and pray for any other past offense in my life. I find myself living fully in the present moment much more often. I find myself understanding that it is ok and very natural that the people I love are not on the same path as me or even always agree with me. Forgiveness is an internal journey and an internal feeling. When anger and resentment are transformed, they are released; forgiveness is a release of a poison. It's separate from whether you reconcile with the person who hurt you. That is another book.

Protecting the needs of your heart and the pace of your own healing process is honoring your inner light. Once you have forgiven, there is still a certain pace and process to whether you allow that person back into your personal space. Close family members or friends will not always understand this, or support you in this, but remember each person has their own journey in life. Life is complicated, and so are emotions, and being okay with this allows you to live each moment authentically. It helps you to set healthy boundaries, and to do it from a place of love. Once you have forgiven, any boundary you set comes from a feeling of love, and when you move forward in love, only love can be returned. With practice you may even find yourself building bridges between those you love instead of creating boundaries.

I've learned a hard lesson, a lesson I live in gratitude with each and every day. If the actions I am doing do not match my heart, then it is benefiting no one. Remember what I said before, sometimes the person who hurt you is part of your close inner circle. It feels amazing to have forgiven this person, but you may not be ready to reconcile. You may never be ready for this. If this affects a close personal relationship, you can try the following technique. In my case, I decided to say, "Please do not invite me to spend time when he is there, it's just not how I feel at this time." "I am working on my own health, as well as my personal comfort levels, so for now, I will decline to go, but thank you."

You can see here that this is pure love. It isn't just honoring myself, but it is equally loving them. It is respecting personal boundaries while also building a bridge for the person or people to be together without you. It is honoring the process. It's honoring the heart and the soul consciousness of everyone involved even if they don't agree.

When you follow your dreams and your heart, there will be those that will be disappointed and those who will rejoice. It's extremely true with forgiveness too. People you love may expect you to reconcile with someone they love, especially once you have achieved forgiveness, but if it isn't how you feel, that is okay. You cannot please everyone. *When you come from a place of love only love can be returned.*

Be patient with those around you as they're on their own journeys too. They don't have to understand your boundaries or your bridge building process, they just have to respect your pace.

Life's magical experiences, who we are, and our unique place in this world, is so divinely important that to try to wrap your head fully around the concept of how important you are as an individual would blow your mind. Smile and rejoice in your victories. Sometimes you may be the only one doing it, and sometimes you may have a crowd of cheerleaders, but you are never alone - you always have yourself.

TEN

Self-Love

Self-love opens a door for personal bridge building, and self-love is ultimately the way to achieving forgiveness. First, you must have self-love. When you are down, defeated, or sorrowful you need to build your foundation with self-love. Even if you don't have it or believe it, just start with imagining that you do. Imagination is extremely powerful; you've been taught to believe that imagination is child's play, but it is not. The only real illusion about imagination is that you believe it's just for kids. Darker forces do not want you to realize this. Self-love replaces fear, and fear is the only grasp that darkness can use against you.

Imagine that you love yourself and accept yourself so much that you cannot hold back a smile. If you don't feel it, just pretend. Smile over and over. Say the words, "I love myself," over and over. Wrap yourself up with some soft blankets, light candles and stare at them repeating over and over, "Life is for living, and I love myself." Do this exercise every day. If you do, your persistence and practice will open new pathways. You will begin to create new connections in your brain. One day you will realize you have relit your inner flame all on your own. The self-love you once thought you could only get from someone else accepting you, or from their responses or behaviors towards you, was inside of you all along. Are you feeling more powerful yet?

Are you someone who suffers from anxiety, maybe panic attacks? I did for years. I still do but much less often now as I have found my voice, my inner-peace and my self-love. My heart used to palpate, relentlessly pounding on the wall of my chest, refusing to let go of the fear inside of me. I remember that I could feel my ribs moving the bones of my chest and the shaking in my hands. It's a complete fight or flight response. I would have shortness of breath, feel annoyed and sometimes angry. Anxiety can often be triggered by what would seemingly be nothing. Even as a little girl I remember having some anxiety and panic attacks.

When I felt like I was going to get into a conversation where I would be challenged, or I felt as if someone may be upset with me, my whole body used to go into this fight or flight response. I'm not sure why, but my body would shut down. If I was on the phone sometimes I would have to say, "Hold on a second," as I put the phone down. I would have to catch my breath because literally, I couldn't breathe. I tried everything I could to pull myself together but my whole body would be shaking.

I've spent enough time in my body to know that this response is autonomic, not just in my head. It really feels like the equivalent of being attacked by a wild animal or being chased by somebody who wants to hurt you. I don't know if it comes from my childhood when I felt lonely quite often, as if I didn't fit in. As far back as I can remember I was always fearful of confrontation.

Whatever it is, anxiety is something that I had suffered from for years and was challenged to overcome. If this is you too, you're not alone.

The biggest memory I have from the emotional struggles as a child and young adult, was feeling that I never really fit in - not in high school, not in college, not even in my young adult life. It took me until my late thirties to find peace with that. It took time for me to build my tribe of friends, my inner circle, and to become a lover of life. Overall, I rarely suffer from anxiety anymore, but I do overthink. My panic attacks occur less often throughout my life, although I do still suffer from them at times. What do I do? I breathe, and you can do this too.

I breathe in and feel my chest expanding. I focus on my exhale and release my tense shoulders downward, letting my neck stretch and feel more open. Then I repeat this action with each inhale and exhale until I feel better. Inhaling, I will lift my shoulders up towards my ears, and exhaling I will let my shoulders and chin drop down, getting a gentle stretch as I breathe. I also confront others with the truth, when needed, and with self-love. Since I found my voice, I have less anxiety now than ever before. You can practice using your voice by speaking up when you feel passionate about a topic of discussion or have a vision for the world, and you want to share it with others.

When there were days when I would feel down, sometimes I would just sit in my treatment, turn out the lights, put music on, and allow myself to be free of thought, if even just for a few moments so I could experience relaxation. Sometimes we are reminded that there are just days that we feel down, and that is okay too.

It's authentic to admit to this human experience. It's okay to have self-love and gratitude, yet still have your days of deep reflection on life.

Anxiety is a strange feeling, especially when you're someone who has so much love for yourself and others, and so much gratitude and pure joy for everything in your life. Personally, I look at my life, and I see all the good. I see so much good it's overwhelming. Even in the midst of all the joy and happiness, I can find myself caught in moments of fear or doubt. It's not unnatural to feel a general sense of malaise, and fatigue. If you think that everyone who is happy and at peace, is always upbeat and joyful, you are wrong. It's not the human experience to constantly be happy, so be easy on yourself.

To achieve self-love, you must teach yourself to lighten up. That's a big part of being able to feel the sensation of self-love. It's a challenge, but it's worth it! You can be an optimist, and full of joy in your heart, and still have your down days, still have your down moments. I want you to know, it's okay. Your feelings are valid, and no matter how lucky you may feel, you have every right to feel how you feel.

When I was a child, I felt a deep sense of loneliness; even when I was surrounded by love I still felt quite alone. I suffered from depression off and on but mostly had a sense of loneliness. I never felt that I fit in. I had friends, but I was never part of a large group and I always wondered why. Now I know one of the important keys to happiness in this lifetime. For everyone, it is understanding that you will not, and cannot, always fit in. It's okay, and it's natural, as we are all built so differently. Love yourself, who you are is perfect.

Want to love yourself more? Then do what brings you peace. If you live to please others, they may be pleased but there will always be others that are disappointed. If you follow your joy, and do what you love, there will be people that are happy about it, and people who disapprove. Either way, the choices you make will always please some or disappoint others. The main difference between the two choices, is that in one situation, you are at peace, healthy, and happy, and in the other, you are miserable. So follow YOUR heart, and YOUR dreams!

About fitting in, and how it makes you feel, let's take some time to look at the emotion of love. Take a moment to think of someone or something you feel love for, through and through. There is such an intense and immense feeling when you think of love right? How much love can exist in our hearts? How little love can exist, and how lonely can that feel? When I think of pure love, I think of the love I have for my children. I love that I have been trained to read between the lines, to enjoy the pauses between the actions of life, and to almost stop time and look at life like a movie reel, watching as a quiet onlooker, as the scenes keep passing by. That is the space where it is quiet, the space where I am always reminded how important every single second is; the pauses, between the inhale, and before I exhale, that I let myself soar in the love I share with my family. It's in those moments when I realize how much love I truly have in my heart, both for my family, and for myself.

> *Love is an abundant energy form.*
> *Love is something that you cannot give freely*
> *to others without first loving yourself!*

Once you love yourself, you can spread this love to everyone around you. You'll be more compassionate towards others, and you'll be more forgiving when someone is unkind to you. You see, The New Forgiveness method isn't just about forgiveness, its starting component is all about self-love. You can rest assured that every single person on this earth responds favorably to love. That includes you! There is a residual effect when kindness is being spread. Not only that, but here's a universal truth for you, even if no one else is showing you kindness you can ALWAYS be kind to yourself.

Speaking of love, who do you love? For me, I love my husband. I love him, our family, and our relationship much more than I love being right. There are times you must choose between the two. Ten years into our marriage the two of us were not only husband and wife and parents to our children, but we were also friends. We loved each other, deeply and truly, but our tough skin and years of digging our heels deeper into thinking we were both right on opposite sides of an issue was quietly and slowly shedding our tight bond.

Exhausted after years of underlying resentment, the crisis of our ongoing disagreement had taken its very last toll on us. The past was behind us but our differing views on how the past should or should not affect our present moment was like a line in the sand - you stand there, and I'll stand here kind of scenario. A clear image of the divide our painful past was still causing was always with us.

I believe that many of you out there are quite a bit like I was for most of my childhood and my adult life up until now. I was generally quick to create boundaries and judgements regarding what was to be done to reconcile a wrongdoing. I would always say to myself, "These are my boundaries." I thought it was healthy to have them, and I had no problem at all finding others who agreed with me, which would fuel my fire convincing me that I was right. The problem with creating boundaries is not the creation of them so much as they are very definitive and create a solid divide. Boundaries are very absolute. Boundaries create no space for error, and in that way, they create no space for error on your side either. There are plenty circumstances where creating a boundary is necessary and self-loving. Feeling that you are "right" is not bad but behaving like you are on a "high-horse" is not good either.

This behavior is easy to identify. If you are behaving in this way, then you know it - you may not admit it to anyone, but you know who you are. It's almost as if when you think of how right you are your chin raises slightly toward your left shoulder at an upward angle as your eyes gaze to the left in a judgmental manner. Did I catch you doing it? It's ok if I did, don't feel bad. Every single experience is there to serve you and to help you grow as a person.

I have absolutely no doubt that the pain and suffering you went through that caused you to put an end to a relationship has its base in good reasoning.

Sometimes what you need is just a bit of patience and courage when you are trying to change the course of a valued relationship in your life. There's a way to think of this amount of patience, as with patience, comes an understanding that you cannot control how fast or slow something changes in your life now that you've made the effort to cultivate that change.

Think of patience like this: you can't push a river, but you can redirect its flow. Literally the pace of an actual river is the set pace of that river at that moment. You cannot stand on the edge of the water and push it so hard with your hands that the entire river flows more rapidly because of your efforts. Applied to life as a metaphor there are just some things that come when they come, and be as they may, whether you worry or not, whether you push it or not, and whether you ignore it or not. Some things just are the way they are.

Don't feel helpless just because the river of life is flowing too fast for you to catch your life's breath, or so slow you feel you can't move fast enough. You do have the power to redirect its flow and because of this you are not helpless or hopeless. Simply put, a beaver can build a dam to redirect the flow of water. People can dig trenches and build dams to create new arms of a river, creating a new landscape entirely. Redirecting the river of life is pure artwork. A little hard work here, a bit of pizazz there, a dash of patience over here and "voila," you've redirected the river and created an entirely new pathway forever changing the landscape of your life.

Life is like this. No one can ever know everything. That means that your perspective and the way you feel about someone, or something is never the full story. Your point of view is the current full potential of your life landscape, and, believe me, it can change, and you have the power to do it. You never know how your perspective can change when you agree to change yourself, if even just a little bit.

Life and achieving your inner most desires require a bit of finesse and a whole lot of patience, practice, prayer, and perseverance. Then once you've done that you practice, practice, and repeat some more. Eventually you know the freedom from your anxiousness and have the inner peace from knowing you have the power within you to achieve your dreams. You can do this by learning and understanding when and how to redirect your flow.

After ten years of a disagreement between my husband and me, we had far surpassed being "over it," or tired of it. We had been tired of being at odds for far too long to even call it exhausted. It was to a point of defeat. Sitting in defeat is an interesting place to be, it's not always rock bottom, but it's certainly a place of loss. It means that what you are doing, or how you are behaving, just isn't working. It means it's time to redirect your flow. Look at my case. Ten years of trying to dig my way back to a connection with my husband and expecting that to happen through the expectations I had of him and the tight boundaries I had put up wasn't working. Some of my boundaries were thick steel walls, and believe me, they were sturdy.

I was great at pointing my finger at him, saying to myself, "He needs to understand that his actions need to be a certain way. He needs to understand that if he does it this way then all will be healed." Banging my head up against the same spot on the same wall for ten years had finally cracked some reality into my head. I felt insane - I was doing the same things over and over and over but expecting a different result.

I was thinking one day about my boundaries, I was thinking about how important some of them were to me, how close and how dear I held onto them. At the same time I was thinking how important my husband was to me and to my family, how important my kids are and providing a solid family foundation was to me, and about how I was ready for us to stop the constant backdrop of resentment between us. I wanted to not only stay married, but to do better. Visually I imagined a boundary. How enclosing and protective it is, but how dislodging and separating it is too. I knew the boundaries I had put up were not healing us or bringing us closer, so I needed a new way to feel better and communicate and decided to envision a bridge. The hope within my heart awakened as I envisioned this bridge, my husband on one side, myself on the other.

You must feel love in your heart to understand the value of creating a connection to heal the resentment you've harbored for so long. You cannot skip the healing process and expect your boundaries to be so easily broken. If you are not ready to forgive and let go of your own perspective then you won't be able to build a bridge between yourself and the person you feel has hurt you in some way. If you have even just a tinge of desire to mend a relationship you know it, you feel it, and that is enough to move forward in this process.

As I envisioned that bridge between my husband and me, I immediately saw a deep ravine. The day was sunny and warm, a slight and gentle breeze was brushing across my face as I meditated on what this bridge would look like. The vision was so real I could feel my long hair brushing against my back and could clearly see to the other side of the ravine. I had my husband close to my heart as I created this image in my mind. The day was absolutely beautiful. There was nothing scary or fear ridden about it at all in my mind or my heart. The inner peace was palpable to me, so I kept my eyes closed realizing that something special was happening to my spirit at that moment.

That place in my daydream was quiet, like the calm of nature far away from any noise or nuisance. Both sides of the ravine had a mountain that led into a forest in the backdrop behind us. On one side there I stood with the forest of trees behind me. I looked down and I couldn't see the bottom of this deep ravine. We were so high up that it must have been ten or maybe even twenty miles deep. I peered across and about a mile away, on the other side, was my husband. He was standing there peacefully, but also looking mighty eager to connect with me. Would I set him free, or would I bind him in some way to my journey with use of guilt or fear?

I could see the love in his eyes and the desire for a reconnection to once again be made between us. In my heart, I had already built the bridge, I just needed him to want to catch it as I tossed it to him on the other side. He did, he caught it, and we both walked halfway to meet each other in the middle of the bridge. We agreed that we could not always go on each other's life's journeys together, but that when we returned, we would always meet in the middle of the bridge. We agreed to stay together. In this moment, it no longer mattered if I agreed with some of his choices. It just mattered that we would be there for each other as we both continued to navigate life as individuals and as a married couple.

When I talk about building bridges, not boundaries, it is in reference to certain scenarios. There are plenty of times in life that you must put a boundary between yourself and a person who hurt you. What I am here to tell you is that I found out that there were times in my life that I mistook the need for a boundary and created it when I should have been building bridges. It's hard to explain because you won't know the blessings of this process until after you have the faith to create it, but I can tell you that the blessings that creating bridges to repair the relationships in your life can bring to you, are far too great to fully imagine until you have done it. One must   experience the rewards of this process to understand it.

> Building a bridge to heal a hurt is like repairing a connection between yourself and another person. It is finding a way to accept that you disagree about something rather than severing your relationship because you do not see eye to eye. Accepting that you do not agree is also a beautiful form of forgiveness. This form of acceptance allows two people to share a bond and relationship while still being on two sides of an issue. What it really does is give the necessary and much needed space each person needs, and in this way, allows them to experience a bond with much less judgement and resentment getting in the way.

The value of an experience or situation you go through is never lost or useless, so keep spreading your love and keep shining brightly to everyone around you, not despite your experiences, but because of them. The happier you are, and the happier you make the world, a happier world it will be for you too. When everything is wonderful in life, you can still have a sense of discontentment at times. You have permission to have a multitude of feelings that are constantly changing. You can be full of gratitude and lust for life yet have your times of sorrow. It is okay! It can be confusing when you have so many opposing emotions at the same time, but this is normal. It's okay to feel blessed in your life, and still feel that somehow, you're missing something. When you feel that you're missing something, you probably are. I don't believe that anything is put into our hearts that is not intended to be filled.

Why do you light up when you see somebody dance? Why do you get goosebumps when you see somebody helping a child on the street? Why do you get choked up watching a touching commercial about suffering? All these feelings are there to serve us. If there's something that you desire, then the universe intends to fulfill that for you. You will have the avenues and the tools you need to achieve it. Being inspired and moved by your emotions is a form of energy. Remember this. All emotions come with energy attached to them, and therefore are a form of energy. You can use this to your benefit, no matter what the emotion is.

If you can't let the emotion go, then
transform it, redeem it. Use it as your fuel
to achieve your dreams!

Self-Love

Experts confuse simplicity.
They take simple concepts,
then use big, rounded words,
with long winded explanations,
just to disguise their own vulnerabilities.

Do not judge yourself on your ability to understand others.

Whenever you feel like you don't fit in, it's ok.
You can never fit in to every circumstance.

You are unique and wonderful as you are,
designed explicitly to fit in where you do,
so you can grow and inspire, where you are,
and when you are needed the most.

"Caroline Pena"

*"Darkness cannot drive out darkness,
only light can do that. Hate cannot drive out hate,
only love can do that"*

Martin Luther King, Jr.

ELEVEN

Achieving The New Forgiveness: How to be a Master Forgiver in 7 Easy Steps

Achieving forgiveness is a process. The most important thing to know before you begin is that forgiveness is a feeling that is inside of you. The feeling of forgiveness is a feeling of internal freedom from hatred, resentment and fear that you can only fully value once you are basking in it. Forgiveness has everything to do with how you feel and has nothing to do with the other person. Once you have forgiven someone, most certainly it may impact their lives as well. You may even decide to reconcile with them, or you may decide to never meet again. Either way, the forgiveness, well, that part is for you.

The second most important thing to know about forgiveness is that forgiving someone for their wrongdoing is not saying that what they did was okay. This is the part where most people fail at achieving forgiveness. They cannot let go of believing that if they forgive someone, it is in some way saying that what they did was okay. Sometimes you may feel that hating someone is the only way to make them continually "pay" for what they did. No one lives in your body. No one feels what you feel upon waking, or in the dark of night. No one else suffers at the hand of your emotional turmoil. Forgiving allows you to feel better in your body, happier upon waking, safer in the dark of night, and in the end, creates a whole new space in your heart and mind to move forward in life with love, not fear. When you are full of love, your entire experience of life begins to change for the better.

Step 1: Notice - Acknowledge - Feel

Notice what happened to you and acknowledge how it makes you feel. Allow yourself to feel that emotion to the fullest. If you are full of resentment, admit it. If you are angry feel it. If you are sad, dive into it and be willing to look at your emotion so intently that you can immerse yourself into the way it feels in your body.

Step 2: Harness your emotional hurt into a ball of energy.

As you feel that emotion to the fullest, imagine that emotion as energy growing inside of your belly. It is growing like a swirling ball of bright white light, almost ready to explode right through your fingertips. Stand up! Shake your body, let that energy fill every corner of you.

Step 3: Use that ball of energy. You have energy now!

Quick, make a call to volunteer somewhere. Hurry, go for a workout, or put your feet in the grass and breathe in that sweet breath of life! Do not wait! Use this massive ball of energy to sit and write that book, or business plan, or create that website. Whatever you've been too "tired" to do, do it now!

Step 4: Use your voice!

Recognize that what you just achieved comes from the energy you transformed from your pain. Say it out loud right now "Thank you!" Find your voice by speaking out and overcoming your pain, with persistence, desire and love. You have achieved one of your greatest goals, because of the power behind the hurtful actions of someone else. You used that energy!

Step 5: Forgive

Recognize that you could say "Thank you" to the person who hurt you, for without the pain they caused, you would not have achieved being the person you are now or be living your greatest vision.

Step 6: Meditation

Do "The New Forgiveness" Guided Meditation in chapter twelve of this book. You can also find an audio version of this meditation at www.CarolinePena.com and on www.youtube.com - Caroline Pena.

Step 7: Vision Project

Do the Vision Project in chapter thirteen of this book, not only is it fun, but it is quick and easy to do. Putting your vision on paper inspires you, and your deepest desires. It places the longings of your heart, visually, in a position to inspire you daily. Even if you do not consciously read your vision heart every day, you are passing by it, viewing it even from a distance, and subconsciously making choices in your life that will be leading you to achieving your vision.

Reconciliation

Forgiveness does not require reconciliation. Feeling within yourself that you are ready to or not ready to reconcile with someone who hurt you is not a requirement to forgiveness. The reason is that, simply put, forgiveness is a feeling you get to have. It's a freedom of the weight of hatred and resentment that you once stored and that now no longer affects you. Forgiveness is a powerful "letting go of the past" and a momentous "moving into self-love and joy." You can forgive someone and see how their actions lead you to your greatest achievements, and yet still not feel in your heart that you want to reconcile. You do not have to welcome anyone into your life or personal space unless you feel you are fully ready to that. It is ok and natural. Do not hold onto this need to reconcile in order to feel you have mastered forgiveness. You are there. You've done it! Your heart is free, your tears have served you well, and now you can soar my friend.

The New Forgiveness Method

Trust your desire for peace and the power of the emotions created by your experiences.

Forgiveness isn't just about forgiving somebody because you are told to, and forgiveness isn't letting go just because you believe you should. Forgiveness is more than that.

Forgiveness is, and can be, a real true and tangible reality in your life. You can begin to understand that the moment that brought you to your knees, to your darkest place, was the moment that brought you forward to your greatest glory.

TWELVE

Guided Meditation: 'The New Forgiveness'

W e will be going as deeply as you can into the trauma that caused you to feel you could not achieve forgiveness. This is the doorway to the other side of your pain. ***The other side of forgiveness is peace, and the other side of hatred is love.*** When you replace the resentment and hatred inside of you, with the powerful energy of love, you can now feel the rewards of forgiveness. That's what forgiveness is, transforming one emotion into another, so you can feel better in your body, mind and spirit.

I have written this meditation to assist you in your forgiveness process. This method is for everyone, from all regions of the earth, all religions, beliefs, races, environments, social constructs, and concepts. If you are reading this, you are part of humanity. If you can transform your hatred into forgiveness, imagine how your life and new perceptions will begin to transform the people and the world around you.

This mediation is best experienced if you can have a close friend or family member read it to you. You can also download an audio version of this meditation, guided by myself, at www.CarolinePena.com.

Get yourself comfortable. Either sitting up or lying down. Make sure your body feels completely supported and that you are not in pain or have any unnecessary tension in your muscles or joints. Let's begin:

Close your eyes, and take a few long deep breaths, breathing in, inhaling…. Breathing out…. exhaling…

Again, breathing in….., breathing out. On your exhale, relax your shoulders away from your neck, and let any tension go by imagining you are releasing your stresses. Create some space between your head and your shoulders, and just begin to relax your body more and more with each breath.

This is a meditation on transforming the energy of your negative experiences, into energy that can be used for good. You are safe now. At any time, you can pause this meditation and come back to it when you are ready. Keep breathing. Long comfortable inhales, let your belly rise. Long exhales, let your belly fall. Begin to think of an experience in your life that caused you to resent someone or feel hatred in your heart. Notice fully how this emotion feels in your body and your mind.

If you are clenching your teeth or jaw, relax. Create a gentle separation between your teeth and relax your lips. Feel a gentle relaxation of your facial muscles as you continue to breathe. I will be your guide through this forgiveness journey.

As you breathe in, connect with your body. Use a childlike imagination to believe that you can connect with your entire body. Keep breathing. Notice how that emotion of hatred or resentment makes you feel. How does your body feel? Where do you feel these emotions in your body? Do you feel it in your head, or in your stomach? Do you feel the emotions in your heart center? Where do negative emotions live in your body? It's different for everyone.

Now, forgiveness. Notice how the thought of forgiveness makes you feel. No feeling is a wrong feeling. Just notice how forgiveness makes you feel without judging it.

Continue with this imagination exercise by using your childlike imagination to follow my instructions and travel through your body with your mind and breath. Inhale and exhale...... inhale and exhale again...... all the way down to your feet and bring your attention to the tips of your toes. As you inhale, breathe in from your toes... and follow your breath from our toes all the way up to your mouth. Really feel your emotions and continue to notice and honor the energy that has built up in your body from this terrible experience in your life.

As you breathe in, breathe into the backs of your knees, into your thighs, into your lower back and feel the weight of your experience becoming lighter as you exhale. Feel your hands and your arms resting. Feel your back connect to your shoulder blades. Feel your elbows, your neck, the back of your head and the crown of your skull. Feel your body beginning to relax and let go, as you breathe in .... and breathe out......

Feel all the folds and wrinkles of the skin of your face, and the skin of your ears. Feel any tension that you have in these muscles and begin to release your muscles and relax your face, relax your ears...

As you're breathing, relax your tongue off of the roof of your mouth. Slightly separate your lips again and separate your teeth so that you are not clenching your teeth together or tightening your tongue, and just, well, let go.....

I am going to take you through your experience so you can harness the energy from it. So you can find the energy behind your pain, and regain complete power to transform from fear into joy.

I am going to count backwards from 10 to 1, and I want you to imagine the 5 minutes before you felt hurt by a situation in your life. Imaging the 5 minutes before that happened, when you were calm and at peace.

As I count back from 10 to 1, I want you to imagine from 10, that you are 5 minutes before that moment. When I get to 1, you are fully in the moment where that situation caused you pain, stepping completely into that moment, of disappointment, of fear, of attack, of being looked over or stepped over, used or abused. Let us begin.

10, breathe in ... you're unsuspecting and you have no idea what is going to happen. 9, 8, 7, the situation is now happening, and you're realizing how angry you are, how fearful you are and how out of control you feel. 6, 5... all of that anxiety, tension, fear, anger or hatred is engulfing you right now, as if you are in that moment. 4,3,2, 1... you feel the anger, you feel the hatred, you feel the fear, you feel like you have no control over something that is causing you so much hatred and pain........

Remember, you are safe. You are remembering a traumatic experience and your body's cellular memory is reacting... you are safe. Take a breath, breathe in...... deeply, then exhale... deeply. You are safe.

Relax your body as you exhale and begin to notice how much energy these emotions create in your body. Imagine that this negative energy, is a gigantic whirling ball inside of your belly. Imagine that it is a massive ball of light, like a clockwise turning storm of electric pulses just spinning in your belly. .... **and notice just how powerful this ball of energy is.**

Breathe into every inch of your body. Breathe into your fingertips, breathe out to your toes.... Again, breathe into the crown of your head, and breathe out, into your belly.

Now, begin to imagine that this ball of energy in your belly, is JUST ENERGY. Imagine that even though it was placed there from trauma, that it is still just a ball of energy, but this energy all has a lot of energy! It is bright, and good, and powerful, and there for your use, at your will!

It is a bright, bursting, white and gold, electric, and powerful ball of energy, just ready to explode!

Imagine that you have a smile on your face.

You realize that you have so much energy built up in your

body.

Imagine that you can use that energy for good!

You have just contained a ball of energy... one sometimes referred to as a qi ball! You are powerful and strong. You can now choose how you harness and use this energy as a special gift, just for you. You can now transform your trauma into good. What will you do with this qi ball of whirling electric energy?

Breathe in...... breathe out..... breathe in....... breathe out......

This ball of energy, while created and driven by an emotion of trauma, hatred and circumstances in your life that were so painful you could never imagine forgiving anybody for doing it to you, is now the powerful force inside of you that you can use to transform into good actions for yourself.

What is your vision? What do you dream of? With your eyes closed, hold this ball of energy inside of you, and envision your greatest desire. Relax your jaw even more. Relax your eyes, and let them sit gently in their sockets, like a hammock of relaxation for your weary eyes.

You can use this energy now.

You can volunteer, do a dream heart board, create, and get excited about your vision, search for that perfect job, whatever you want to do.

You now have the energy for that which you never had the

energy for before. Harness that qi ball inside of your belly. Use it to achieve your happiness. Use it often, and the more you do, one day you'll feel thankful for the one thing that almost broke you and your ability to forgive.

Begin now to understand that this ball of energy is just energy. Neither good, nor bad, just energy. As you continue to breath, feel your belly rise and fall, and right now, you have empowered yourself to harness and control the greatest energy on earth... the energy from your emotions.

Relax now... have you been tired? Have you been fatigued? Have you wondered how you could ever get past something terrible that happened to you? Now you can. You have this big, beautiful, electric, lightening type of energy that you can do anything you want with now.

You can stay with the ball of energy, and leave it in hatred, refusing to let go, or you can take this energy, and use it as the fuel, as the propelling force, your fire, to move forward in a positive direction in your life. Think of one thing you've wished you had the time or energy to do, and imagine that you are doing it, that you pursued it. Imagine what doing that one thing would look like. Imagine what it feels like to have the amount of energy it takes to pursue that dream, that goal, that moment, that peace of mind.

Now imagine that you're taking this big bright ball of qi, this glorious amount of energy you have harnessed in your belly and focus on something good. You pick up the phone and you make a phone call that you want to join that team, or take that job, or move to that other state, or call that neighbor you've been wanting to go for a walk with, or do a long bike ride, maybe do some volunteer work, or do some charity work that you never had the energy for before.

Now, in your minds-eye and imagination, do it! Imagine that you're doing it. Imagine that you get up off of your couch, or your chair or your bed, and you make the call, or you make the move, or you create the idea, or you begin writing that book. Imagine that you take that energy, and you shift it, you create something great, because you have a lot of energy right now! As you move forward, almost instantaneously, you'll begin to feel thankful for the experience that made you feel so much hatred in the past......yes, thankful, ...keep breathing....

Why? Breathing into your experience gives you energetic power over it. Without that experience, you would never have had the energy to move forward into the direction of your greatest cause, of your greatest movement. Let that which got you down, be the force that lifts you higher than your dreams! Breathe in..... exhale.....

Now I am going to count you back up, from 1 to 10. When I reach 10, imagine that the energy from your trauma is now the powerful, beautiful force that awakens you to the inner joy, peace and happiness that you've always imagined you could have. Now you do!

1, 2, 3.... Rising up through your breath, bringing that energy ball of qi with you,..... 4, 5, 6......., 7 starting to awaken and move your body, 8, 9, 10... burst out a breath of victory, open your eyes.

That is forgiveness.

THIRTEEN

Vision Project Awaken Your Vision – Achieve Forgiveness

Y ou may have heard of a creating a vision board or affirmation journal. The purpose of this vision project is to awaken your vision and create your new reality, one that encompasses forgiveness. When you put your dreams, visions, and desires down on paper it creates an actual picture for you to see every day. If you put your Vision Project on your refrigerator, your bathroom mirror, in your car or maybe at work near your desk, you are encouraged daily to remember to repeat your dreams in your mind.

The more you do this, the more you create the actions necessary to make your dreams come true. Subtle actions can lead to great change. My family and I have been making dream board's every year for about eight years now. I can tell you that almost everything we put on our boards becomes a reality that year. Some-

125

times it's as simple as us looking at the board as a reminder that we need to accomplish something, so we make it happen.

A Vision Project is powerful. I ask you to make it in any shape that inspires you as a constant reminder of your visions and dreams. I chose to do one of my Vision Projects in the shape of a heart, because my greatest visions come from my heart, and the greatest energy in your heart is love. Your Vision Project is a reminder that when you move forward in love, only love can be returned.

1: Find a piece of paper. Take your time to pick a color that inspires you.

2: Cut it into your favorite shape, large enough to use for VISUAL inspiration. I recommend a minimum of eight inches or bigger.

3: Around the outer edge, write in all the roles that you happily play in life. Example: Mother, Daddy, Friend, Neighbor, Boss, Son, Daughter, Husband, Visionary, Athlete, Lover of Life, etc.

4: Now, hold this paper close to your own heart and close your eyes. With your eyes closed begin connecting with your vision. Use your imagination to "see" your heart's greatest desires.

5: Think of three things that inspire you or drive you. Think of what you want your life to look like. (You can do as many as you want, but please do at least three.) These three things are YOUR visions. They are how you see your life, the world, and how you see your here and now. This is your present moment, or your vision for the future. All answers are correct here.

6: Now draw these visions on your colorful paper. You can write words or draw pictures. It is YOUR vision and YOUR art. So listen to YOUR heart as you do this project.

7: What you put on your Vision Project will be your new path. Be honest here and let your emotions and imagination soar. Let it flow and be brave. You are creating your now.

You are creating your future. You are already living your vision by doing this Vision Project.

Sample Vision Project

The heart you see here is the Vision Project I created while in the process of writing this book. Igniting your vision inspires the pulse of joy inside of you to come out and become your reality. I did it when I started the journey of writing this book. They are things I envisioned that I wanted to do, achieve and believed in. Now do yours and let your visions be seen and become reality.

127

FOURTEEN

Conclusion to The New Forgiveness Method

The New Forgiveness method teaches you how to identify, harness and use the energy from your emotions. You've learned that you can use the pain caused by your trauma and transform your daily experience of that emotion into joy, inner peace and self-love. Life has its many twists and turns, so does the process of transforming your emotions into forgiveness. I have written this book to assist you in your journey back from your pain, and into once again realizing you are a powerful force, so powerful, in fact, that you can forgive.

The first step to any healing journey is restoration of hope. Now that your eyes and hearts have been opened to the energy around forgiveness, you can now be hopeful that forgiveness is possible. Remember, when you see things through a slightly different lens, there is an endless world of possibilities that you are now awakened to. Your suffering is real, and so is your ability to heal from it.

"Sometimes we think there's no way we can live with or find peace with a hurt after something that has happened, but we can. If you don't believe that, the darker forces have you right where they want you. Forgiveness is possible."

Achieving forgiveness is becoming a master of letting go. Once you have forgiven that which you could never have imagined letting go, you will realize that you are now better at it. Once you have forgiven, you get better at it and faster at it, eventually becoming a Master of It. If you completely accept that you cannot have a better past, then happiness will soon follow. You'll no longer dwell on the past and what may have been, and realize that you can only move forward, and how you choose to do so is up to you. The New Forgiveness gives you an avenue to achieve this. It's a new way of understanding forgiveness and gives you the tools to let go and let yourself be fully happy once again.

Forgiveness requires patience, practice, prayer and perseverance. Then you practice, practice and repeat some more. Eventually you will know the freedom of forgiveness. Forgiveness ultimately takes the ability and deep willingness to let go, to be opened to letting go, and to see yourself as your best and highest version of yourself.

Dedications and Acknowledgements

To my husband Cesar. Thank you for letting me be me. Thank you for forgiving my shortcomings and teaching me how to embrace happiness. Thank you for allowing me to constantly change careers and follow my dreams. You are a stellar dad, a magnificent husband, and you are my friend. I am forever in gratitude, for the life you have made with me, and for me. Thank you for loving me, as I know how deeply you do. Here's to the poem you wrote for me when we first met. "My love for you is the bond that keeps my mind, being, spirit and matter altogether. Without it, I would be scattered in pieces." I love you.

To my children, Maddox and Sarai. You inspire my soul, you drive my dreams, and you ignite my love in ways I would never have known without you. You are my biggest and most cherished of all life's gifts. You are forever and always my greatest achievements, and you are so very deeply loved. Always be kind to each other. You have a sibling, and you can guide one another on life's amazing journey.

Regina, Leigh Anne, Shelley and Johnny, thank you for seeing me, and for believing in me. You inspire me and the world around you. The respect I have for you is deep and evergreen. You all are my greatest and most cherished gifts. Some of the most amazing parts of my life are because you have been an integral and influential part of it. You are a blessing to me.

To my Mom, my Dad, and my sister, Tammy. I am grateful to be a part of this family. We sure have been down some roads, but the best feeling I have about all of us is that we are still together, in love and acceptance. I would choose no other journey. I love the three of you immensely. We still gather, we care for each other, and we embrace, and we care deeply about the success and happiness of one another. You have been my starting foundation, and as I have grown into womanhood, you have been the ones I think of the most often. To my entire family, and my extended family, my cup overflows with gratitude for you.

To my goddaughter, Julia, you will forever be my sunshine. The world and all of its greatest possible achievements are right at your fingertips. You are deeply loved and it's honor to be your god-mother.

About the Author

Caroline Pena is an award winning author of the book, The New Forgiveness and is the co-host of "The Kindness Project Worldwide," produced by Plumb Talk Productions. She is also a co-host of The Global Vision Conference™ and is available to speak at events as well as offers private, customized, one-on-one sessions to teach and train on The New Forgiveness method. Caroline Pena is a nationally double-board certified Diplomate of Oriental Medicine, Acupuncture Physician, Herbalist and Asian Bodywork Therapist.

Caroline graduated from The Atlantic Institute of Oriental Medicine in Florida with a master's degree in Traditional Chinese Medicine, and a second degree of Bachelor of Health Science. Caroline received her first Bachelor of Science and Humanities from The Ohio State University and is a member in good standing with FSOMA (Florida State Oriental Medicine Association) and NC-CAOM (National Certifying Commission of Acupuncture and Oriental Medicine). Caroline runs her own holistic medicine practice in Palm Beach County, Florida, Holistic Health Palm Beach. She can also be found at www.CarolinePena.com for details about

The New Forgiveness Method. Caroline offers The New Forgiveness Method coaching sessions, shares downloadable guided meditations, updated blogs and more.

THE NEW FORGIVENESS

All rights reserved

Published by:
Global Vision Publishing
Fort Lauderdale, FL

Copyright © 2022 Caroline Pena

All rights reserved. No part of this book may be reproduced by any means, nor transmitted, nor stored in a retrieval system, nor translated into a machine language, in any form or by any means, electronic, mechanical, photocopying, recording, or otherwise, without the prior written permission of the author.

Caroline Pena • www.CarolinePena.com

Global Vision Publishing • www.GlobalVisionPublishing.com

Cover design: Tim Pedersen
Cover photo: Plumb Talk Productions
Editors: Tammy DiBacco and Carrie Lyons

Printed in the United States of America

ISBN-13: 979-8-9857948-7-8

ISBN 979-8-9857948-7-8

90000>

9 798985 794878

www.ingramcontent.com/pod-product-compliance
Lightning Source LLC
Chambersburg PA
CBHW030305130626
46549CB00002B/711